Th)
of Brian??

Brian Krishnan
Illustrated by Kai Tavender
Edited by Kevin Krishnan

The Real Life of Brian??
Copyright © 2025 by Brian Krishnan

All rights reserved. No part of this publication may be reproduced, distributed, or transmitted in any form or by any means, including photocopying, recording, or other electronic or mechanical methods, without the prior written permission of the author, except in the case of brief quotations embodied in critical reviews and certain other non-commercial uses permitted by copyright law.

Tellwell Talent
www.tellwell.ca

ISBN
978-1-83418-134-9 (Hardcover)
978-1-83418-133-2 (Paperback)
978-1-83418-135-6 (eBook)

In Memory and Dedicated to Brian John Krishnan (SNR) AKA Butchy
07/03/1946 – 20/01/2005

This fish is called "Butchy", which looks like there is a word "DAD" on its side.

This rose is named "My Lovely Dad."

A Star that was named after my Dad, Butchy.

Introduction

THIS BOOK IS BASED ON the life of my father as I saw him. He was not only a father to me, but also my best friend, work buddy and above all, my idol and a hero second to none. I probably got to spend a lot of time with him, probably even more than my ma.

As the years went on through my life, it became apparent of what an incredible man he truly was. If I could be part of what my father was, then I'd be happy. His boots will never be filled for sure.

I never had the chance to show and express just how much of a great person in his living years, as his modesty hid much about him. He may have come across very mysterious and reserved, but many who knew him could tell you stories about him that would raise many a brow.

From my memoirs, I hope you will see what an amazing man he was. Even though he was deprived of a life very early, he just got on with things. He never gave up and never complained about the rough hand he was dealt with in life.

The Early Years

I SUPPOSE LIKE MANY, READING back in the memory banks of early childhood memories was difficult for me. Silly things can jog the memory, sounds, smells and songs being the main instigators of this.

I can go back as far as maybe four years old. Some memories are like bubbles, you reach out to them and suddenly they disappear. I can remember silly little things like when we were on holiday and my dad taking me on a swing that was in the sea, you see, like that bubble, it just a vague memory that disappears like the burst bubble. At around the same time, I remember sitting with my sisters on the balcony in the hotel on one of our first holidays, that unforgettable taste of fizzy orange and spaghetti Bolognese. Orangeade always takes me back to that time.

I also remember flamenco dancers with castanets and pretty dresses, dancing in loud shoes and the song 'Viva Espana; as though it was yesterday, but other memories are only retrieved with greater thoughts. I even remember my dad taking me to a stable where he towed me around an arena on a pony. He had a great passion for horses. For not only did his father have a horse, he enjoyed horse racing, greyhounds too for that matter, much to my mum's displeasure. She would often nag him about going in the bookies.

Even though he was quite small, he was confident around them. He would often take me over to the fields near where we had a caravan at Selsey Bill. He would call them over and then lift me up onto their backs and then slap their hind, so they would gallop off. I didn't look very dignified that's for sure. He teased me one year, I remember when we went to the new forest and we came across a few wild horses, one was a mare with a foal. He teased me and said "Shall we take it home", you could not imagine just how excited I was! I was disappointed when I realized that he was just pulling my leg, but I know in my heart that it'd be best for the foal to stay with its mum.

Besides even though it was only a small foal, it was never going to fit in the boot! He often told me that my grandad had a horse and cart, and he kept chickens and also reared canaries.

Another memorable moment which involved horses was when we went to Wembley to get tickets for the F.A. Cup Final replay, it was 1990 I believe, between Manchester United and Crystal Palace. My Dad was a devoted Man United fan and I was born in South Norwood where Crystal Palace was the nearest team, so it was the perfect final for us, I used to go to Crystal Palace with my primary school mates. It was like an adventure to get a 157 bus to Selhurst.

Back then, kids could sit at the front of the advertisement boards, we'd buy roasted peanuts and have a drink in the plastic carton and straw, normally a rank orange tasting drink that they also sold in the cinemas as I recall.

So, we were queuing up for tickets, when suddenly it was announced over the public announcement that all the tickets were sold out for the replay, and that we had to go to Selhurst Park. There were many supporters from Manchester that had come down to get tickets and there were lots of murmurs of disappointment from the crowd. With that, a man with a pony tail pulled out a massive wad of tickets on the steps by the ticket office and he shouted "Right! Who wants a ticket?!?" With that a group of supporters rushed him to grab his tickets off of him, causing a frenzy just feet away from myself and my dad.

They were holding him to the floor and a policeman came to his rescue, who was mounted on his horse, he was manoeuvring the horse to shield the man and were getting caught up in the bustle. My dad threw his arms up in the air which made the horse rear up!

The funniest thing happened next, when a load of fans took the horse whilst the policeman aided the ticket tout! He then realized what had happened, but because of the multitude of people there, he couldn't see which way his horse went. He was jumping up to see, shouting "My horse! My horse!"

Some of the supporters started making neighing sounds and it added a bit of amusement to the situation to be fair. My dad just grinned and then chuckled. What could have been a naughty situation was down played by him making things not so bad. He explained to me that throwing his hands up in the air was a good way to stop a horse in its tracks!

So, it was off to get tickets at Selhurst Park, that was my job for the day. Queuing up in an endless line (getting paid for it mind you!) My dad was very passionate about football and he'd always want to have a kickabout when there's a football about. He was always trying to get me to play football, but I was not overly interested in it, to be fair, my love was fishing.

However, I used to enjoy participating (If I was permitted) on the parents' football match that was scheduled on a weekly basis at our holiday camp in Selsey. Dad wasn't a bad footballer to be fair, but he had a dirty side to him, resembling 'Chopper Harris'. My dad underwent football trials and he claimed he was okay up until he had a serious knee injury that finished his chances of playing on a professional level.

I remember one particular game I was allowed to play in goal and my father was playing in defence. A great big man who must have been well over six foot, went to come into the box with the ball and my dad chopped him down. To say he wasn't very happy was an understatement. "What are you talking about? I went for the ball!" he retorted, but he enjoyed it nonetheless.

We even played as a team against other building contractors once. We dressed in Juventus kits and the others were dressed in Real Madrid kits. It was hilarious! We came marching out of the basement like pros. Shamefully, we lost that game! And guess what? My dad suffered an ankle injury for a fifty-fifty ball, well according to him it was! I'd say it was the last time that he actually played a serious game of football.

Another thing I remember was my dad's eagerness to make my sister and I famous, looking back now, I understand why. For he came from a big family, with lots of siblings and didn't exactly have it easy. He was sent to boarding school and life never dealt him a fair hand. He worked hard as an electrician and with fate turning some comfortable outcomes for him and my mother (which I will explain further later) I fully understood he wanted the best for us.

He was a self-employed electrician who went from pillar to post. One day he met Sylvia Young, who was a modelling agent, one of the best in fact. She asked if he had kids and any photos of us. This was the start of our careers in various T.V. commercials and photography work. I was a bit cheekier and more forthright than my sister, although she was and still is, very pretty which showed in her photo shoots. I was fortunate to get chosen for T.V. adverts, which I felt was due to my lack of shyness.

I really don't know how he managed it, but we started at a stage school where we learnt to dance, well, I did! My sister Lorraine could already dance and I think she could have gone on to Italia Conti dance academy as she was a fantastic dancer.

My dad would also be our chaperone on most occasions. He'd be standing in the wings, grinning, like the Cheshire cat! He was so proud of us. I managed to do a few adverts but decided one day that I didn't want to end up a spoilt brat, it was not for me. He was very disappointed. He would still try his luck when we would have mysterious application forms come in the post for things like 'The Clothes Show' auditions. You had to love his persistence.

Like I say, I do understand why he did it. I'd still do a few turns on the stage, as I mentioned before, I liked acting the clown and used to do a few impressions and normally finished off with a song. The good thing about those, is that I could do it when I wanted to!

My dad's worst side in my eyes, was with the lack of care to the maintenance of his cars. He would break down in the most inconvenient places possible. He would often run out of fuel, or water and once he even seized his car for its lack of oil. But we would break down in the most unthinkable places. I think he had a low regard for most of his cars, except his Mini Cooper. All the others were just deemed as worthless. But even work horses needed maintaining, which he needed to be reminded of. I think both my sister and brother, and even my Ma, had experiences for the worst surrounding his cars, which was surprising as he taught my sister and I how to maintain our cars.

I could think now as I write this, of at least three cars, he had, where the petrol gauge was not working on them. He used to drip feed them enough fuel in order to get from A to B, but was quite often miscalculated, sometimes admittedly it was where he just simply didn't have much money.

One time we broke down in Railton Road, in Brixton. This was known as 'The Front Line' and a 'No-Go Area'. But oh no, we broke down, or should I say, ran out of petrol…..again!!! It happened a few times in his car, as it was one of three cars where the gauge wasn't operative.

You'd get that tell-tale splutter from the engine where it fought to stay running as it scraped the bottom of the tank. You'd hear him tut, "Shit!" he'd say. Yeah! Shit all right! Can't we at least run out near a petrol station? He'd crawl as far as he could, then he would push it the rest of the way to a suitable place in kerbside. He was strong for a short guy, I tell you!

"Don't open the doors to anyone!" he said and off he'd go with petrol can in hand. I used to duck behind the front seats and wait for him to return. I often wondered why he left me, now as an educated guess, I'd say it was in case a traffic warden came, so they would take pity on us!

Like I saw, he probably broke down the furthest point you could be from a garage or any salvation. I remember another time at Knights Hill, again a dodgy place to break down. Again, I would assume my position behind the front seats. One time he genuinely broke down right at the function of Tibbets corner, approaching the big roundabout. "Christ almighty!!" he said, he said that quite a lot actually! I heard something give way. Bloody typical! On a Friday too! Pub night for me.

One thing my dad was great at, was improvising. He found a coil of cable in the boot that was thick enough and long enough to run to the clutch lever. Somehow, he managed to run it back into the car and eventually he had a make-do mechanism, or at least he thought he did. It had some force to get it into gear, but eventually the cable gave way where the copper was just too soft!

To say it was embarrassing was an understatement!

Cars were bibbing him; he'd cuss back at them. It was so painful! He'd resorted to Plan 'B' where he timed getting the car from first to second gear, by dropping the revs and crunching it in gear. The journey seemed endless. We got home in the end.

By far the worst occasion, was when we were returning from a job near Aldermaston. His poor little Nissan Micra came to a halt quite inconveniently by the Wisley interchange on the junction of the M25. He managed to get the car down a small slip road. Great!!!

My mate Gary was meant to come to work with us that day, so I decided maybe to give him a ring as he was good with cars. I recalled there was a phone box the other side of the carriageway on the A3 by the lake there. So, my dad tinkered with the car whilst I went to the phone box. I crossed over the foot bridge, passed a lorry lay by, then sure enough, there was a phone box. I was praying Gary would answer, and as luck would have it, he did!

I explained to him what happened, and where we were. He was always helpful and he said he'd come straight away. I explained that I would wat by the roadside and wave to flag him to get off at the Ripley turn-off. So, I made my way back to my dad. As I passed the lorry lay by, I smelt perfume. I looked around and up at this lorry, but couldn't make them out as the Sun was falling and was blinding my vision. All I could see was a silhouette, so I carried on walking and thought nothing more of it.

I got back to the old man who was still tinkering under the bonnet. So, no luck there then. "I got hold of Gary, so I'm going to wait at the lay by to flag him down, Dad". I spoke.

"Ok, I'll keep trying the car, he said".

Light was fading fast, so was my patience. Luck was never on his side which it came to cars, for he'd fall in a bucket of tits and come out sucking his thumb! I got back to the lay by and I stood and waited over the other side of the carriageway for my mate Gary. He's got to here soon, surely? I took a sip of my Lucozade and glanced at my watch.

Suddenly a 4x4 pulled into the lay by. I glanced up and saw a silhouette of the driver who seemed to have curly hair. It was now dark, but it was safe to say it was not Gary. The car started flashing its indicators, then all of a sudden, the driver got out of the car. You could have knocked me down with a feather! The driver had a PVC top on with two holes where tits were poking out! Dressed in a mini skirt and donned in fish net stockings. Not a sight you see every day of evening, eh?

The driver then went to the front of their car, in front of the headlights. To my horror, I noticed they had stubble. It was a man! I turned into defensive mode and gestured to them with my Lucozade bottle that I was going to crown them. All I could visualize was Fredde Mercury when he did the pop video for "I want to break free", where he was dressed up as a woman with stubble.

I think my body language came over loud and clear and the driver got back in their car and drove off!

Suddenly, I heard my dad shouting "Now look! Fuck off out of it!". I was like a rabbit in headlights. Amongst the commotion, I managed to get a glimpse of my mate Gary on the opposite carriageway, so I gave him a wave. My dad came marching up the slip road, hands clenched

into fists and a concerned surprised look on !
he blurted out "You'll never guess what hap

I replied "You'll never guess what happ
was just approached by a geezer dressed in drag.

"Well, I've just had a man ask me if I was going his way!". I added.

"What did you say?" I replied.

"What do you think I said? I told him to fuck off!". dad added.

And with that a car came up the slip road with a man leaning out of his window.

"Look! Fuck off!" I said.

My dad shouted, gesturing to hit the stranger. The man then sped off, after blowing us a kiss.

Gary pulled up in the lay by just in time. He couldn't believe it when we told him what had happened. So, we went down to where the car was. I held the torch over the bonnet for Gary as he started to investigate what the problem was.

Suddenly, I heard a rustling in the bushes! I quickly shone the torch over to where the noise was coming from.

It was a man with his small dog that was dressed in pink bows, he was walking like he was strutting up and down a cat walk.

"Keep that torch over here for fuck sake!" Gary said.

I cracked up, for I'd never see Gary looking nervous, he was quite a stocky bloke.

"Look at him! My dad exclaimed.

Then ANOTHER car drove by with a couple of men inside, one had a Rasta hat on and bright lipstick.

"Let's get out of here!" Gary said. "I think the car is knackered, I'll tow you home!" he added.

Dad said, "We will have to come back with eggs or paintball guns!".

That's got to be the most memorable breakdown event I shared with my dad. It wasn't the last either and I'm sure Gary never forgot it either.

My dad wasn't homophobic to be fair! He told me stories about two of his mates, back when he was younger, who were transvestites. He also used to take my mum to the Vauxhall Tavern when they were courting, which was known for its gay punters.

That breakdown story was reverberated many times over the years and it brought a smile to my face when he sadly passed away. It brought surprise to others, that never saw that side to my dad. And no, we never went back down there with eggs or paintball guns.

I started to see a different side of my dad when I started working with him. I saw a skilled side to him, and also how diligent and hard working he was. How could a man that had lost his child through such a tragedy, have the strength to carry on as he did?

He was hardly ever off through illness, even when he showed pain from the cancer that would be his nemesis.

I spent so much time with him, probably more than my mother did to be fair. He taught me many tricks of the trade and I could see just how much respect he had from others, which many would have a high regard for him.

He first started me taking me on little jobs at first where I mainly used to muck about throwing stars out of crampets or playing dangerously with the Hilti gun cartridges. They were like bullets. He'd often get cross with me for, as he said, "Pissballing about!". But my first real job was Dorking District Council Establishment.

It was a proper building site and I used to feel so grown up sitting in the canteen with all the other tradesmen. It was here that I tried to work on metal conduit for the first time. My dad used to beaver around the vice and bender like a gymnast on a pommel horse. Using the arm to bend the tube around the former and putting threads on the tube. He made it look so easy and he'd tube with one eye, make a little adjustment.

"How do you do it?!" I asked. "Can I have a go, dad?".

"Yeah, you can do" he said.

So, I got all eager and he asked me to put a double set in a bit of tube. Well, I jumped and bounced on this arm to put a bend in, but to no avail! I was way too small and light. For I was only thirteen years old and back then, I must have weighed only six stone. I knew that because I was boxing then. I tried the way my dad bent it by putting a foot on the frame of the bender, but to no avail. He just grinned.

His grin spoke a thousand words to be fair. I was lucky to be on site really, but he used to have an incredible talent by blagging and he would even believe his own lies, little white ones.

I also found out just how dangerous sites were too on here when the bricklayer/labourer on the site decided to empty his wheelbarrow down the stairwell which contained bricks and rubble. My dad pinned me to the wall suddenly, shielding me from the falling debris!

"Oi! Oi!" he shouted. He went ballistic.

This particular labourer was a nightmare! Wasn't the sharpest pencil in the box for sure and looked like a caveman. He often wore cutdown shorts and worked without a top on. He'd have cement on his hairy chest, a proper animal and would sometimes sit opposite me scoffing a bit of bread-and-butter pudding that had an inch of fat on the bottom in a very vocal manner. So much so, that it would put me off of my breakfast! Sometimes his runny nose would spread across his tea, I still cringe at the thought to be honest, even though it was 40 odd years ago, it seems like yesterday.

Little did I know, that my dad was hatching revenge. I just didn't realise how vindictive and vengeful he could be! Years back then, each trade had their own site hut of office and my dad got wind this this labourer called Dick had been having murders surrounding his holiday being cancelled by the travel agent, Thompson Cook. How my dad thought of these plots was beyond me, but he schemed a belter! So, he rang the bricklayers portacabin and asked to speak to Dick, stating that he was from Thomas Cook.

"Hello, is that Mr Richard *****?" Dad asked, in a well spoke voice?

"Tis, yes" Dick replied.

"I'm sorry to inform you that your holiday has been cancelled!" My father added.

"Do what?!" said Dick and promptly hung up.

Apparently, my dad saw Dick marching up Dorking High Street with his hod on his shoulder.

Poor Thomas Cook!

I think it was my dad's way of getting even. He very much believed in an eye for an eye.

He often used to say "Take me for a dime and I'll catch you for a dollar".

I suppose that's where I got it from. I remember my first job as acting foreman, he carried out his worst case of revenge out of malice that I could remember, and for good reason too. I was overseeing a small team of five electricians, my father, Gary (who I mentioned previously), Eddie, Stevie and Sean. To be fair, they were so good and the job was running automatically.

We were running to a programme, or was meant to be, but the site agent, John, had other ideas, he turned out to be a nasty bit of work. He would deliberately try to muck up my programme, he would screed outside rooms that were due to be conduited or trunking installed. He got so nasty to the point that I lost my temper with him.

The site was around two hours away from my home. One day, my partner text me that she was up the hospital with our baby daughter who had suspected meningitis. So, I rushed over to John's office and asked if I could use his phone. Without looking up from his paperwork, he replied "There's a phone box down the road!"

Although I was his spitting image and had a lot of Dads ways, I got my temper from my Mum. I was fuming! I pulled him out of his chair and roughed him up against the wall. "You horrible bastard! My daughter could die!". He was shaking like a shitting dog! I used the phone anyhow. That was the final straw and John conveniently took a week off of work. Following that, I went home or went to the hospital, fortunately my daughter pulled through.

Our battles continued onwards after John returned. Don't people ever learn? I think he knew not to push me too far, but it was fair to say that he was still a dick. I don't understand why because we were progressing well and making him look good.

One day I asked John if he could get the large pile of rubbish taken away, that was left by the canteen. It was really stinking. "Do it yourself!" he said? OK then. So, I poured a load of PVC glue on it and lit it. Now the gloves were off! "I'm really going to gun for you now matey" I thought.

The job was nearly at the point where I had to start laying off the other sparks, coming up to Christmas too, made it very difficult to do. If only I could keep them until after Xmas! The boys knew it was drawing to an end; it came with the territory of being a 'subby' but still hard for me nonetheless.

To say that I was a chip off the old block, was an understatement. I couldn't tell you the number of times I've heard "You an 'arf look like your dad!". I got to admit, sometimes, I look in the mirror with sadness and see my father, as it is painful not having him here. Although I was like my Mum in my behaviour as a whole, I adopted a lot of my dad's ways too, his vengefulness was one of them.

All I could think about was getting even and I'd heard of jobs that are subject to sabotage, so this was the stance I adopted. That'd teach the bastard! It sounds a bit harsh, I know, but I can't tell you how much he tried to muck me up. So, an eye for an eye, seemed only fair. But how could I get revenge?

I eventually came up with a plan to flood the job in a way that no fingers could point to anyone, so I took the split pin out of the float from the main water tank in the roof space of the building. The float would eventually come loose and the tank would continue to fill and overspill, causing a massive flood. It was just a matter of when, not if. The anticipation was reminiscent of waiting for the fireworks to go up.

Unfortunately, to my disappointment, my plan was scuppered as the plumbers discovered the split pin malfunction. They came into the canteen and I overheard them talking about it.

"Good job you noticed that split pin had worked loose, that could have been disastrous!" I heard one of the plumbers say.

"Bollocks!". I muttered.

"Don't worry. I've undone the compression gland on the inch water main" my dad whispered, raising his eyebrows and peering over his paper.

It was like he knew, a mind reader.

I can't tell you how long it was after that when it happened, but it did! And in style too! What I do remember, was leading up to Christmas, one of the other sparks was working in the loft when all hell broke loose. He was working diligently and hard as usual, when the pipe blew apart! He jumped up pretty startled and banged his head on one of the beams. The water gushed into the trunking that ran around the perimeter, it cascaded out of the conduits and looked like a massive water feature on the ground from our view up in the roof.

The labourer ran to get the site agent. Poetic justice! As he entered the building, the ceiling caved in due to the weight of the water. The site agent dropped to his knees. I wasn't sorry one bit! Not only did it look like an accident, I could keep my labour on until after Christmas because all the circuits had to be isolated, dried and tested, before it was deemed safe to be switched on. My turn to be in control and I loved it!

It was on this job that I saw the nasty side of my Father and I could see why he adopted the nickname "Butchy". His heart certainly made up for his size. One thing I did differ from my dad, for I grew to six feet, probably taking after mum's side, as my grandad was a big man, and is my Uncle David.

The tension on the site was detectable, so much that the head plumber got so frustrated that he got all aggressive with my dad. "Oi cunt! When are you going to switch on the power!?" I heard him say.

Uh Ok! Defcon one! I could see my dad moving towards this huge man with his hands clenched! I had to get there and stop him! He was moving towards the plumbers that were seated around this hydrotherapy pool. I cut across on of the other entrances and got there just in time!

"Get out of my way!" My dad said with clenched fists and gritted teeth".

"Calm down!" I spoke! "Get back" I added to the plumber foreman.

I could see my dad trying to get within striking range.

The plumber foreman moved back towards the edge of the pool and by the other soaked plumbers.

All of a sudden, one of the plumbers jumped out of his seat. To be fair, I think he was trying to just get out of way! With lightning speed, my dad cracked the plumber on the chin, knocking him backwards over his chair and nearly into the pool. Shots fired!

Somehow, luckily, I managed to defuse the situation. I think the plumber foreman realized that he'd come unstuck. We were called into the office for a meeting, although the fight constituted a dismissible offense, it was deemed that we needed to stay so that the job could be finished. My dad laughed and commented to me that the bloke he hit resembled Prince Andrew!

The job eventually got finished, and the other sparks who we worked with on other jobs afterwards, often reminisced about that job. All three spoke very highly of my dad, which made me very proud. In fact, I met many who said he was a good man and great at his job. We had a few jobs where he showed his ugly side or I did. But it was mainly over being protective of me, that he would show his nasty side.

One job we got the sack because he clumped a bloke because the guy picked me up and threw me against a big armoured cable drum; I was rolling on the floor in agony when dad walked around the corner. I was only 15 back then. It all started when I'd gone into the canteen, put my packed lunch on the table. I'd bought a sandwich and a bag of plums from the market. I went to the toilet to wash my hands and when I came back, someone had taken nearly all of my plums out of the bag.

"Right, what funny fucker has had my plums?", I shouted

"I did!" this bloke shouted at the hot counter.

"Well, you might as well have the other!" I replied and threw one bang onto his chin.

His face immediately changed. Uh oh! Time to leg it. I bolted out of the door with this geezer hot on my ail. I zigged and zagged to avoid him. He was like a man possessed. Suddenly, he managed to get hold of me and picked me up, then hurled me through the air.

This would be the first job that I got kicked off, but not my last. I think on that job, I realized what a jungle the building site could be.

I spent countless hours that amounted to years, working with my father. Countless bangs on my bedroom door to get up for work. How did he do it? It dawned on me that he was a machine! But he had to. For suffering a tragedy and then having to work harder as my beloved mother gained a serious injury to hear back, resulting in her being unable to work. He was destined to work for the rest of his life, to provide for us. Another thing I began to realise, and part of what made him so great.

Even when he injured himself at work, and believe me, he had some terrible injuries, he'd still be trying to work. One day he nearly cut his thumb off with a wood saw. I would have said, "Sod that, I'm taking a few days off!", but not dad. Most times he'd even negate going to hospital. To say he was accident prone, was a fair assumption.

I remember one day that he had to go to the hospital after I hooked his nose with a barbed hook whilst fishing. I reckon that was one of the main reasons he sacked off taking me fishing, as I am devoted to fishing even to this day. It was when he was working in Dorking and he used to drop me at the River Mole some days and collect me on his way home. I never wanted to pack up and would say "Last cast!" and he'd reply "Come on! Your mum has got the dinner on". So, I gave it one last cast and I overshot it to the far side and got caught in the overhanging bushes.

I gave the rod and line a firm tug and it came flying back towards my father who was walking back up the bank, so I tried to avert hitting him. Suddenly he put his hands over his face and I looked at the end of my line to discover that there was no hook. I glanced back at my dad, who still had his hands over his face.

"You soppy bastard!" he growled at me.

I must have turned pale "Sorry dad!" I exclaimed.

"I'll give you sorry! You could have had my eye out!" he added!

Phew! Thank God that wasn't the case. As he moved his hands away from his face, I noticed something black sticking out of his nose. "Shit!" I thought, it was my hook!

"I'm really sorry dad" I said. Only the shank of the hook was showing and it was a barbed hook. The hook had imbedded itself deep in between the bone and the cartilage of his nose. He kept trying to tease it out and I even tried getting it out with my disgorger too, but to no avail.

He tutted and said that we'd have to go to the hospital end route to home. So, he drove to St Heliers hospital accident and emergency, frequently glancing in his rear-view mirror at the hook. Dad was quite vain. I sat sheepishly in the front seat and silent too. We got to the hospital and he said that I should ring ma and tell her where we were.

The waiting room was really busy and the phone was on the wall in the corner and not in a booth, so I know was going to beard by the other patients in the waiting room. So, I put my hand over, to cover my mouth and try to muffle my voice from carrying too much.

My mum answered the phone "7307".

"Hello ma, we're up the hospital" I said.

"You what? What's happened" she said

"Don't panic, but I've put a hook through dad's nose!" I explained, in a soft and calm voice.

"You've done what?" she shouted.

"I've hooked dad's nose" I repeated.

My reply was met by a few giggles and sniggers from the waiting room, by eaves dropping patients. I glanced over to my dad, where I was met with a dirty look. "Oh gawd, I'm in for the high jump", I thought.

Dad was eventually guided into a cubicle, where he was told to lie down and injected with an anaesthetic, so that they could operate and remove the hook. The injection made his eyes water and I said to him "Don't cry dad!"

"You'll be crying when we get out of here!" he said.

A cross was cut in his nose to remove the hook and he was stitched up and was now ready to go home. As soon as he got back to the car, he was straight on looking in his rear-view mirror, gritting his teeth, turning left and right profile.

"Sheesh, Jesus Christ Almighty" he muttered and that was the end of it.

I dare say that he got his own back on me. In fact, we shared a lot of experiences where we would injure each other unintentionally.

I recall one time we were working together in a house; it was having a full rewire. One of the bedrooms had a few layers of lino down so it had to be removed I think it was fair to say that I was accident prone, just like my father. I used the crowbar to get the floorboards up when all of a sudden it slipped off one of the old floor nails and I took the bottom of my chin out with the end of the crowbar.

"Come here! Let me do that you're going to hurt yourself" he said. So, we used these claw hammer to de-nail the board.

He gave the hammer of whack at the top of the hammer shaft with his hand and it came flying toward me hitting me square in the face. I thought at this point I was doing a better job myself!

"Jesus Christ!" he said and tutted. To be used to make a fuss too much and never pampered me when I hurt myself, I think it was just his way. I sometimes wondered at times why he brought me up like that, I think it reflected on just how hard that he had been brought up. I suppose that's partly the reason he adopted his nickname. My grandad would often address him as Butch'.

I can think of numerous occasions where he watched me take hiding in a fight. I copped to proper hiding once outside a nightclub and I should have listened to him when he advised me to follow them when they came out as opposed to confronting them at the nightclub exit. This is where I took after my ma, for she did most of the fighting.

Her temper would go from cool to psychotic instantaneously, whereas my dad was calm and collected. There were numerous occasions where he would watch my mum scrap over us kids, boy Could she fight too! One time she had a fight with a man who was headbutting her, she gave just as good back though. I was furious when I found out, and I still don't know to this day who the culprit was.

It sounds bad about my father; he felt things were in control. Sometimes they reminded me of Bonnie and Clyde, I remember 1 occasion, my dad got jumped by six or seven big blokes in Wimbledon. I'll never forget it! I was 8 years old and my oldest sister and I were in the back of the car. The rain was biblical!

As he came down Wimbledon hill, a group of men approached a crossing, but my dad was unable to stop safely as my mum was about due to have my baby brother, she was nine months pregnant, I was eight years old at the time of the incident. As he drove past the group of men, a couple hit his car so my dad stopped the vehicle.

The men surrounded our car refusing to get out of the way, my dad revved the engines to try and get them to move, to say it was a scary moment frost was an understatement. Failing to move the man in front of his car, my dad jumped out of the vehicle. This was the first fight that I saw my dad involved in.

All the men surrounded my dad, they all towered over him. By this time my sister and I were screaming at them! Then all hell broke loose.

My mum got out to help my dad, her fists started flying, she was something else my mum. I still remember screaming and swearing out the window, to leave my mum and dad alone. Eventually the police turned up and Congress restored once more. No charges were made, even though my mum had knocked out one of the men's front teeth, it turned out he was a Harley Street dentist too. Irony at its best?

My parents sustained only minor injuries; my dad was in a neck collar for a few days and my mum had cuts on her knuckles that's it. I think the police must have looked at my mum being so heavily pregnant and my dad being attacked by these men and thought…..seriously?!

The only other memorable time I remember my dad fighting was over me. I was only 15 at the time, but a full-grown man's jealousy got the better of him as he thought I fancied his girlfriend who worked at holiday camp as a children's entertainer. Apparently, the boyfriend thought I stuck my middle finger up at him, which was a good enough reason to headbutt me on the nose.

So, I ran into the bar, took off my jacket and handed it to my Ma in the saloon bar.

"Hold my jacket!" I said with blood streaming from my nose.

"What's happened??" Mum said.

I rushed out back out the door to catch up with him, unbeknown to me, my dad was in hot pursuit behind me!

"Oi! I ain't finished yet! Party to him, as he turned round, I threw a right-hander at him which caught him square on his jaw. 'CLONK!'.

Then from out of nowhere, my dad steps in front of me. His fists started like pistons. All I could hear was this man's head hitting the wooden cladding. Luckily for him, the security came to his rescue and he was taken to safety. Serves him right deserved all he got. I think I was more stunned seeing my dad's reaction. I definitely did not expect that!

The police turned up at our caravan. The first of many times I might add! D13 was our caravan number, which must have haunted the owners of the caravan park. I was asked to give a statement of my account of what happened and it turned out that the attacker who was 10 years older than me, was meant to be going to Australia. Because I took my coat off and then attacked him, I was cautioned and warned that I had committed an offence by going back and fighting instead of defending myself. You gotta love the law, eh?

By now reading this, you must be thinking, Jesus! What a family! But as you will read there was a different side to us. I came to the conclusion that my dad just couldn't bear seeing me upset. One time, I fell over in the snow. My own stupid fault really, walking up an icy slope with both my hands in my pocket I mean what would I think would happen? Of course, I slipped and fell on my face, before I could get my hands out to brace my fall, and put my front tooth through my lip.

Being vain like my dad I went straight to the bathroom mirror, moaning and not crying. Suddenly my dad appeared in the doorway. He clipped me around the ear and said "there's something to cry about!"

"But I wasn't crying!" I exclaimed.

I recall actually getting a sorry out of him one day which I was quite shocked about, as I stepped into a left jab of his when he used to spar with me, as he took me boxing in my early teens.

"Oops sorry but you stepped into that one!" he said. The nearest I'd get to a cuddle.

I knew he adored us; he just had a funny way of showing it.

For in the years we've spent together, we only had a couple of tiffs if you like. The biggest one I remember was when we were still working together on a building site near Brentford, I think I was in my late teens and it was a usual building site, very noisy. I was asked to identify cables in the concrete box as they were not identified, and I was meant to pull certain cables so that my dad could fathom out what they were.

He was situated the other side of the wall, inside the building. I was located on a set of steps in the entrance to the building, like I say it was very noisy, bloke beside me using a Kango drill and I could barely hear my dad.

"Right! Pull the red one!" he shouted.

Apparently, I pulled the wrong red, and the cable came out!

He came to the entrance and shouted at me "You soppy cunt!"

"Who you calling a cunt?" I replied.

I think he was shocked that I actually came back at him.

I was so annoyed that he said it in front of an audience, So I threw his car keys to him.

"Right! I'm going home!" I announced.

"But you ain't got no money" he said.

"I'm going to walk!" I added. And off I went, cursing and talking to myself on route

I didn't mind a yomp to be fair and I was going quicker than normal because I was in a temper.

Ended up getting near to a bus service that went towards home as I had enough money just for one bus journey so I managed to get to something, after which are carried on walking to Wallington.

I was still mumbling to myself when I got home. I laugh when I think about it now.

When I got home my ma said to me "where's your dad?"

"Where is he? Miserable fucker! He's still at work".

I told her what happened she just shook her head. A few hours later, my dad arrived home and I could hear him talking to my Ma.

He came in the front room on looked over, raised his eyebrows with gritty teeth. It wasn't a growl or snarl or a smile, more so a sheepish look.

"You coming to work tomorrow?" He said.

"No I'm fucking not! Call me a cunt?!" I replied.

"Come on come to work" he repeated.

Still no apology.

I knew that was the best II was going to get from him. I did eventually fold and give in, and went to work. That's the biggest fallout I had with my dad; he was like my older brother most times. He called me a 'Soppy bastard' once when I shut his head in the boot of his Toyota Celica once. It was like a film scene out of Laurel and Hardy or the Three Stooges. Although I was a little upset that he swore at me, I think it warranted it as he rubbed his head. I can honestly say that they're the only times that we never saw eye-to-eye. We had a special bond and it went back to the tragedy that hit our family when I was five.

We even worked abroad a couple of times, I loved that! My dad would let me drive his car whilst he'd read his paper, which he loved. I'd get told off a couple of times, as he would look up and I'd be booting it down towards Dover. He'd bark at me to slow down and then carry on reading.

We rewired a little cottage not too far from St Omer. It was a quiet town called Cassel, the people were really friendly and they would try to communicate, even if they couldn't speak English. My French wasn't too bad to be fair. This part of France was occupied by the Germans during the second World War and there were many graves of soldiers situated there, which made me feel very humble. The streets were cobbled and a lot of the buildings had bullet holes strewn across the facias. It seemed like time stood still there. Everything looked so antiquated and houses were untouched for decades.

After we finished the cottage, we had to renovate a place, not too far from the cottage in Cassel. All the locals called the place "Le Grand Chateau", which translated in English means "The Big Castle". It was being converted from a place where the Germans occupied, to a restaurant. We were working alongside my dad's eldest brother, Alan, his other brother Buster, and his mate Frank. They were workaholics!

We'd work until six or seven o'clock sometimes. I'd hoist their arms in to stopping on one of the cafes for a beer or two. Everywhere in town closed early, sometimes the barman would be falling asleep on his beer taps.

"C'est ferme?" I'd ask in French, meaning are you closed?

To which he'd reply "Non monsieur!" and would offer to buy us a drink.

Customers would also talk to us in broken English, matching my broken French.

There was a great little shop that had a rotisserie too and the bakers did delightful cakes, but you had to get there early as it closed around four.

I even tried to find a nightclub, but realized just how primitive this part of France was, when I found out their equivalent was a barn with flat beer in polystyrene cups, playing really outdated music.

We were not that far from the Belgian border, so we'd cross over and my dad would get cheap cigarettes and tobacco. It was a lot less expensive there and my dad would make a few quid here and there to pay for his and mum's cigarettes. I used to feel really humble going to the

Menin Gate at Ypres, where they played 'The Last Post' in memory of those lost during the wars. I visited there in Easter time too, which they seemed to celebrate more than us. The cakes and chocolate were amazing there too. Many people would be dressed up in custom, it reminded me of a carnival, people carrying lit torches, beat drums or blew trumpets. It almost seemed a shame to go back over the border.

We'd work over there for a few days, up to two weeks on occasion. My Uncle Alan never knew when to put his tools down, my dad would be telling him to hurry up so that we would make the ferry back. I remember one time they were rushing to get a particular job done and Frank was cutting a bit of plywood, whilst sitting on the side of it with a wood saw. Suddenly, it snapped in half and sandwiched him to be met by laughter from us. Now they had to pack up! So, it was a rush for the ferry port at Calais.

I hated this bit as I knew full well that my dad would have too much over his allowance for customers. He was such a blagger that he would even drive through 'Nothing to declare'. You could see in his car; he was clearly over the limit. The Toyota hatchback was like a greenhouse with wheels and stuff was clearly visible in the boot.

One trip home, we had been stopped back at Dover, as usual my dad had driven through the 'Nothing to declare' section and the car was full to the brim with alcohol, beers and other merchandise. Unbeknown to me, he had bought a lot of it for my surprise birthday party. Poor Dad, got collared to pay the tax on the excess alcohol! His car was like a magic box, he got asked whether there was any more in the car that he forgot to declare. He'd reply that there wasn't and the officer would lean in the car and find yet another bottle of booze stuffed under the seat. I think it still worked out cheaper than buying it all back at home. It didn't deter him from doing it again either.

He got stopped one day coming back from Turkey with ten thousand cigarettes apparently. My mum was going ape about it, she never cared that they were carrying guns. They led my dad away, but only as far as the cashpoint, as they were happy to accept a bribe! My sister said it was a bit of a scary moment. She said mum wouldn't shut her gob and thought dad was being arrested!

The New Chapter

As mentioned earlier, I recalled only a little of my childhood memories; it is likely that this is due to a defence mechanism, designed to block out the major tragedy we suffered as a family when I was five.

It would be fair to say that none of us would be here, had it not been for my eldest sister, who alerted my dad of the looming danger, the house fire that sadly took my little sister away from us all.

I remember opening my bedroom door and then locking it again after I confronted the road of the fire. My dad actually broke into my bedroom to save me. He had to carry me through a wall of fire, across the landing and down the stairs. He was only in his pants and I can't imagine how he managed to get us out.

I remember my mum running up and down screaming and trying to get back in to get to Gillian, who was still upstairs. The smell of smoke has forever been etched in my memories. I still to this day, am repulsed by the smell of smoked bacon as it sets off all my triggers and I get flash backs. I recall being dazzled by the lights from the fire engines.

The fire was that bad, that not even the firemen were able to get to my sister. She was gone forever. How did my mum and dad carry on? They had hardly anything.

This to us, was a situation similar of that to the poor people of Grenfell. It was easy to relate to those who experienced such tragedy. Where would we live? What about all our clothes and toys?

I do remember staying with our nan and grandad for a spell. As I mentioned before, I remember silly things like flowers that smelt of pepper in my nan's garden. I also remember playing and cuddling their black Labrador, Tina. One of my uncles also had models hanging on string too. I can even relate to smells of boiling vegetables, which still take me back even when I smell them to this day.

I think it was there that my happy childhood memories stopped for a while. We ended up getting rehoused on the Stockwell park estate which unfortunately wasn't too far from where we had the house fire. We have recently found paperwork and correspondence from my dad to Croydon Council, requesting a move. The only thing I remember when we moved to Stockwell, was playing with my Scalextrick set and my weeblecopter. I also remember my dad taking down to Hamley's in Cold Harbour Lane, Brixton, to get a new car for my Scalextrick set. I also remember being really ill with tonsilitis and stupid as it may seem, our Wombles Pillowcases, one of the few things that survived the fire. My mum had to beg for some of the belongings as she clutched onto precious things like my departed sisters Jack-In-a-box. Which we still have. To think my dad and mum still had to function, despite such a tragedy.

Our paths of life finally changed when our family got an offer of a move to Wallington. These were new houses that had been built opposite our square where we lived. We had barren, feral, untouched land where apples and pear trees grew, blackberry bushes and ample other trees for climbing. Definitely a culture shock to what we were used to.

Was this going to be a brighter future for us?

We were to start at a new Primary school, and I'm laughing as I write this, because it was the first memory I have of meeting a boy, who became one of my mates that I grew up with. Bobby was his name, and our first encounter was him shouting "Bollocks!" through a grilled that was on the side of the school hall, that which I will never forget. Bear in mind that we were only 8-9 years old, I liked Bobby because he would eat all the stuff on my dinner plate that I hated.

Our school wasn't that far away from our new house. My eldest sister and I would use to walk together. We would meet our new friends on the way to school, the boys getting up to the usual mischief, which I liked to call harmless fun. Knock down ginger (knocking on a front door and running away) was an obvious choice of past time to us young lads. The odd scuffle, but mostly we got on really well and continued to do so as we grew up. Fonder memories were made, amongst the hurt and bad memories that still brandished us all in different ways.

My ma, as to be expected, would suffer with depression in peaks and troughs. Being put on Valium, was not the best of decisions as it rendered her into a zombified state.

We would normally tell what mood she was in, whether she was up or down, by the type of music that she would play. If it was music by Harry Nilsson, "Without you", I would want to walk away as we would often be met by the quivering lip and telling tears of my mother.

My sister and my encouragement of love and affection, was not enough to bring her round. It would not have only benefitted her, but for my sister and I too. Lorraine would often love to 'play mum', we morally supported each other. I think we had a stronger bond that most siblings may have, and we still do to this day. She would often help me get my stuff ready for school. We would often play together; I'd have my soldiers and she would have her Sindy dolls. We acted more like twins to be fair; we shared a weird telepathy.

There is only eleven months between us in age, but Lorraine's maturity was miles ahead of me. Just as well, for my dad would often have to work later, he had to. He had to provide, not only for my sister and I, but for my Mum too.

I would often wait for the key in the door to be met by raised eyebrows. His tongue would normally be poking out, latching onto the side of his top lip. He was a man of few words really, be had a thousand expressions. I'd be met with the odd "Hello BJ", sometimes his eyes would roll if Ma was in one of her down moods. Most times he met her with a kiss on the cheek and a "hello lovey".

Dinner was normally time to that of the arrival of my dad. Then he would normally make a beeline for a cup of tea. To say that he loved a tea was an understatement! I'd be very rich, if someone gave me a quid for every tea that

I made him. When I worked with him, he would make a letter 'T' with his hands and he'd be grinning. He wasn't much of a drinker of alcohol to be fair, my Ma made up for him in that regard!

When he did drink alcohol, my dad's tipple preference was a Bacardi and coke. He may have started on a couple of beers, but he'd always end up on his Bacardi. He would come out of his shell and become very unpredictable! I even heard that he got up on stage and sang, which I couldn't believe when I heard! He would like I dance that I know, but he was really shy. Apparently, he did a rendition of 'When you're smiling' (Kev edit, Daydream believer as well). To even get on the stage would have been something for him, let alone sing!

I hadn't hardly heard him sing, he liked a whistle and a dance. He loved his reggae, ska and blue beat. He was a Stones fan too, and he loved Love Affair's 'Everlasting love'. It often brings a tear to my eyes when I still hear it now. He was funny, seeing him dance to reggae, he used to pick me up and dance with me when I was a toddler. Seems mad really, as my ma loved her rock and roll. They shared a lot of common ground musically, with The Searchers, and Del Shannon. Mum would often drag dad up for a drive or a slow dance on the dancefloor, at the ballroom, down in Selsey.

The Happier Years

Although my mum would always give my dad stick for "Always being in the bookies", it was his good fortune on the horses that drastically changed our fortune for the best. Despite what my mum thought about my dad constantly gambling, I don't recall that he would spend too much time in the bookies as I worked with him a lot.

He would pop in the odd time, but I think financially he wasn't able to constantly gamble like she said he did.

She had more vices than he did to be fair, his financial instability due to being a standalone self-employed electrician made it very difficult to keep a regular cash flow. Numerous times over the years, he was 'knocked' for monies owed, or suffered being laid off due to a couple of recessions. One time leading up to Christmas, my beloved daughter was only about 8 weeks old and we hadn't been paid for two weeks.

The boss had just come back from Rio and had only left cheques for his employees and not self-employed people like us. I was desperate for nappies for 'Little-un' and I was sick of seeing my dad getting a rough deal, enough was enough! So, I encouraged him to go to their office and get our money owed.

When we got there, I caught one of foreman in a garage on the side of his house, which he used as an office. He had nowhere to go, I made it plain to him that we weren't going anywhere and he needed to get the boss out. He kept trying to blah us that the cheques were issued, which was a lie.

"I swear to God, I'm going to hurt you If you don't go and get the boss out!" I snarled.

"And I'll be taking all this stuff in here, too" I added.

He went into the building to get the boss and he locked the door. I knew in my head what was coming next. Sure, enough in the distance, I could hear a siren. The fuckers had called the police! The sound of the siren got nearer and suddenly a police car pulled up outside the alleyway.

"Right, what's going on?", said one of the police officers.

"We've come to get our money" I replied calmly.

Upon hearing the arrival of the police, the owner of the business finally had the balls to show himself.

"I don't appreciate my staff being man-handled!" the other barked.

"And I don't appreciate not being paid before Xmas either" I replied

I thought I was being rather diplomatic, as I wanted to grab hold of him and throttle him, but I stayed fairly calm.

"You can't man handle anyone Sir" said one of the police officers

"What would you do if you had an 8-week-old baby with no nappies then?" I asked?

"I think you'd better try and sort this matter out!" The officer said to the boss.

He seemed to realise our sense of urgency.

I was sick of how my dad had to battle to get his hard earnt money and that was the stance I took alongside him. I was sick of seeing him lose in court because companies could deliberately fold up and then reopen as another company or appoint another director.

He would sometimes have to borrow money from banks, just to keep us clothed and fed.

He must have had so much on his plate!

So the one day where fortune had smiled on him and he had a win, he was able to give us a happier childhood. I don't exactly know how much he had won, but I remember he had to go back to the bookies to get a cheque from them! It must have been a fair few bob, that's all I knew!

He stated to take my Mum, Sister and I to various caravan sites to look for a van. He took us to Leysdown, but my ma didn't like it. Eventually we ended up getting a caravan on a holiday camp in Selsey. An eight birth 'Bluebird' as I mentioned before, it had the address of D13.

We were sited just by the side of the Whitehorse club; it had a swimming pool next door to it (Bloody freezing it was too!). It had a local chip shop and prize bingo parlour, and a bike hire where my sister and I used to frequent. They had the double bikes on four weeks, I used to do a James Bond and make it go on two wheels and scare the hell out of my sister. We'd hire it out of our pennies that our nan and grandad would save up for us in the holidays.

nan and grandad would come down for a few days, normally for the weekend. On the odd occasion, my sister and I used to go in their car down to Selsey. It used to take ages with them, his car resembled a Batmobile and he drove really slowly. We used to duck down with embarrassment so that we were not seen by anyone we knew.

Times in the bar and club would be more fun than usual as my grandad loved life to the full! The bickering was so unforgettable between my nan and grandad, going on about what a "Greedy, greedy bastard" he was, as my nan often called him.

Nan would go to bingo with my ma. When she won, she'd make everyone jump by shouting "Right!" instead of "Bingo!". For a tiny, petite lady, she certainly had a set of lungs! She also had an uncanny habit of burping so loud during the most silent of times, especially during a game of bingo. "Manners!" she'd say after a burp, followed by a loud 'tut' from my grandad along with one of his disapproving stares that was one of his trademarks.

Sometimes my dad would roll his eyes, but as a whole he got on with his 'in laws' really well. He occasionally showed his impish side to him, which would land him in trouble with my Mum. One year he gave my grandad Ouzo, neat, which caused him to be very ill. For my grandad loved a drink, and he would turn up at our house enroute to his house from the pub. So, he'd already had a skinful when my dad gave the Ouzo to him. Grandad was the type of man would could drink for England, and drink you dry! When I got a round in, he would drink his light and bitter before I got my change!

This particular day, my dad had not long gotten in from work, when my grandad knocked on the door. We had an inner porch, so dad could see who it was and rolled his eyes and tutted. I think it was because he'd not long gotten in from work and normally liked that half an hour, to sit down. My grandad looked 'half cut'.

"Hello son!" he said and chuckled in a sloshed manner.

"Te, te te, what have we got to drink then?" said grandad after a chuckle.

My dad rolled his eyes again, looked over at me, grinned and raised his brows.

"I'll have a look in the cabinet dad!" he said.

So my dad walked over to the cabinet and opened the doors. Inside amongst the gleaming lead crystal glasses, there were two 2 Litre bottles of drink, one was cider, the other was tartan bitter.

"I've got this dad" he said and showed him.

I don't think it really mattered to my grandad, as he was already quite drink.

"Been at work Butchy?" grandad asked?

"Yes dad" he replied.

They had a good relationship, which said something about the type of person my dad was. They were always winding each other up or playing pranks.

One time, my ma said that my dad had to take my grandad to hospital as his appendix had burst. He had been driving his lorry, so my dad had to go and get him. Apparently, he had to lay him down in the car. My dad said he could hear my grandad crying out in pain every time he went over the bumps. He said it was raining so heavy the car he had, you used to have to accelerate to make the wipers go faster, but in doing so it exaggerated the extremity of the bumps which made my grandad howl in pain.

"Slow down you bastard!" he shouted

He used to grin, my dad, when he told me that story.

So, my grandad finished the bottle of bitter and he'd look over at my dad and say "Are you cold Son?". My dad always sat with his jacket on and my grandad used to give him stick for it.

"Are you going to have an operation to get that off?" was another of his sayings, to which my dad used to grin and raise his eyebrows.

"What else have you got boy?!" grandad would ask dad.

My dad went over the cabinet once more and showed him the bottle of cider.

So he poured him out the cider and grandad soon waded through that too!

I never knew how my grandad could rink so much, he had such a guzzle on him! My a took after him, she even won a yard of ale drinking contest once down the caravan, she did it with her brother David, who couldn't manage it and he had to go to the loo to be sick!

There was nothing left in the drink's cabinet, apart from a bottle of Ouzo. My grandad was well on his way to being completed sozzled. His swept back hair was coming forward, his eyes were drooping and his breathing started to resemble 'Darth Vader', which was a long-standing joke that my brother made up about him.

"Got anyfing else Son?" he said in a slow, slurred fashion.

"I've only got this" My dad said.

"Ooooh wassat?" My grandad said, squinting at the bottle.

"It's Ouzo, dad, all we've got left".

dad forgot to mention how potent that stuff was as he poured him a BIG glass of it.

Who would have thought how potent it was, given how Ouzo looks water.

grandad polished off the lot, neat.

I actually still remember being worried for the welfare of my grandad as he looked really pale all of a sudden and had the legs of a newborn giraffe! He was a big man, with size fifteen feet, but he needed help to get home that day. Mum went ballistic at my dad! I can still see my dad grinning with an impish glint in his eye.

I wish I could say that taught him a lesson, but abstinence from drinking was very short!

I can still remember my grandad numerous times, saying that he had a good time and "How long do you live" was a frequent saying of his. In the end, for the record, he actually outlived by dad, and I had one last drink of brandy with him the night before he passed away peacefully. He even said to me the night before that he had such a good life and that he was ready to go now to see my Nana.

There wasn't only the bar and the club at our caravan site, we also had choices of beaches to go to. West Wittering was not that far away, which was a nice sandy beach to visit. We also had the Lifeboat at East Beach, West Beach and of course, Littlehampton, where we would normally visit in the summer holidays. My sister and I made many friends that owed caravans like us, we would often meet up and hang around in our little crew at the swing parks or over the playing fields.

I can still remember the excitement waiting outside the school gates of our school for my dad, who would pick us up and drive to Selsey for the weekend. Sometimes the car would be so full that we had to squeeze in the back amongst the duvets (mainly on the first visit of the year).

My sister and I would play 'Ring ring, rat-tat' on the way, on a journey that seemed endless sometimes! If you saw a telephone box you shouted "Ring ring!" and you saw a post box, you shouted "Rat-tat!". I sort of cheated in a way, as I memorized where most of them were on the way and would call out just before I even saw them. Sometimes I 'd get distracted by the wildlife that I saw on the way, like a hovering Kestrel or a deer in the fields.

I remember sometimes that we used to stop for dinner at Fontwell before descending into Selsey, but most times we'd race to get down there for the opening of the White Horse club on the site.

It was nice to see my mum and dad actually relaxing, especially my dad. We would go most weekends from Easter, right up until late September before closing up at

Halloween. My mum used to stay for the summer holidays with my sister and I whilst dad worked, eventually my brother also. I still remember waiting for my dad to arrive on site after work on a Friday during the summer holidays, somehow, he made it just that bit special!

Our neighbours next to our caravan were great too. We'd have barbecues that were truly memorable, back then it was very sociable and communal affairs, even people emptying out from the White Horse club would gatecrash them. Sometimes the on-site security would ask us to turn it in, Sixties and Seventies music blaring out and everyone having a great time. The spread laid on was a combined effort and marvellous they were too. We'd have party games and that added to the fun.

I loved it down the van, because we were given that freedom to just go off and have an adventure. Losing a child made my mother be over-protective of myself, my brother and my sister. I would often follow the river that meandered through the whole of the campsite. I'd be looking for all sorts of wildlife, which was a great passion for me. Lizards, adders, grass snakes, as well as birds of prey, that would be looking for their next meal, particularly the kestrels that used to hover above. Hearing the skylarks was a spectacle too, where they would warble an incredible song as they climbed further and further up into the sky, where it seemed like they'd be flying to heaven!

The van was also the place that my passion for fishing developed, which I still very much enjoy. It keeps me sane; it unravels life's knots. Back then I would stare into the shallow waters, looking for the tell-tale signs of the fish moving in the waters. There were mainly eels in there, which were so fascinating to watch as they seemed to dance with each other. It was heart-stopping seeing them approach my bait, as I waited eagerly for my float to glide across the water and the bob under. I developed a technique to stop them tangling up my line! I attempted to wrestle with them, equipped with a cloth. I think that's what put my dad off fishing with me, because one game off in mid-air when he lifted it out of the water and wrapped around his neck.

I used to sell them live at first. I went around from caravan to caravan, in order to find punters to buy them off of me for eating. It paid for replacing lost tackle and also to buy maggots to use as bait. It was more practical and efficient in the end, to gut and cook them myself. I learnt how to make jellied eels and it seemed more profitable to sell them that way. However, it was such a disgusting process in gutting them, that it put me off of eating them in the end! I found it fascinating how they would still move, despite being beheaded and cut into sections. You could even put an eel under a trance, a dormant like state, by covering their eyes and stroking them from head to tail, where it seemed like they went to sleep.

There was an outside tap a few meters from the caravan where I used to gut them. I'd kneel on the eel tail to keep them still, ready to gut them. I suffered one mishap doing it this way, when I attempted to gut one of the biggest eels I'd ever caught. It would have made that eel sadly around thirty to forty years old and it weighted three pounds and twelve ounces. It gave me trouble from the start when I caught it.

As mentioned, I laid the eel by the drain, knelt on its tail and cut off its head with my extremely sharp gutting knife. The head would still move and it gaped its mouth. One of my friends distracted me, whilst I slipped the gutting knife inside the eel, preparing to remove its guts.

"Eeeeew, it's still moving!" my friend said.

With that, I was distracted enough to cut myself across my knee with the knife!

Oh, the joys!

So off to hospital I went. Unfortunately, they could not anaesthetize my knee for stitching, still wince thinking about it to this date.

As I said, this eel was trouble from the start and I caught it whilst night fishing by the archery field on site. This was very good for catching eels, as it was weedy and provided a good habitat for them. My dad used to bring me fish and chips to eat.

Night fishing helped me with a phobia that I had about the dark.

Eventually I got used to weird noises that I heard through the night and curbed my vivid imagination.

I still remember my battery float playing tricks on me, looking like it was moving. But there was no mistaking the float moving with the big eel! It shot across, nearly pulling my small Woolworths fishing rod that I was using. I had no torch, only a street lamp by a nearby caravan. I had to pull with all my might to bank it, but I must say it was easier to handle, it was thicker and longer than my arm! It was OK catching bigger eels, but it was bloody difficult keeping them in the bucket!

I'd put a plastic bag over the bucket, but they had a habit of getting out and you could hear the bag rustling. So, I came up with a hairbrained idea of putting the big eel in the communal ladies' shower cubicle that was sited on the touring caravan section, right by the archery range.

I'd often fish until I dozed off and I couldn't keep my eyes open, so I put this eel in the tray floor of the shower unit for good keeping. Suddenly, I was woken up by a scream coming from the shower unit and ran towards the cubicle to be faced by a lady screaming in her dressing gown! The eel had gotten out and was snaking towards her, she just froze, leaning up against the wall. So, I apologized, pickup up the eel and ran out the cubicle! I won't be doing that again!!!

They were enjoyable times; I moved on eventually when I was old enough to venture further. I started to get a 250 bus from Selsey town centre to Hunston, where I picked up part of the Chichester Canal. They had a variety of other fish there, plus it was a different environment. I preferred going to Chichester lakes at Southern leisure, where I caught my first ever carp. That was truly memorable!

Sometimes my dad would pick me up or drop me off there, if he was going to Chichester for shopping. He wasn't very forthcoming with offering lifts for my brother, my sister and I. Just as well really, the amount of time he'd break down! Plus, he'd stand well back when I casted now too. I loved the canal as there was much more to see.

I'd see shoals of Rudd or the odd Leviathan Carp just cruising slowly past, occasionally I'd get the odd glimpse of the Kingfisher as it flashed past. I always dreamt of having enough money to buy a particular house that is sited on the bend of the canal. It was there that I caught my first Pike too! The pike was quite small, around ten to twelve inches and was quite a surprise as it grabbed my piece of sweetcorn whilst I was reeling in! Truly very happy memories for me.

My mum's best friend also bought a caravan there too, Bill and Pauline were like our uncle and Auntie, their children, Billy, Carol and Tracey, we knew and addressed as our cousins. I remember my uncle Bill participating with my dad in various activities that were held on the caravan site, like a strongman competition. The funniest and most unusual was the drag contests!

I never thought that my dad would dress up as a woman, he was too shy! He even went in for the Tarzan contest where you would have to fireman carry your beloved one. That was easier for my Uncle Bill, as he was a fireman; he let me dress in his uniform once, when I was little. I was that little in fact, that his axe touched the floor. I had a lot of admiration for my Uncle Bill as I wanted to be a fireman when I grew up, sadly I failed during my application as my lung expansion was insufficient, ironic really as you will find out later.

I used to enjoy the welly throwing competition, adults and juniors could participate. It was funny because some adults took it rather seriously and would practice before the competition. The prizes were not game-changers and it would normally finish with everyone going back to the bar where my mum and Auntie Pauline were waiting. It wasn't just us kids that socialized, so did our parents. They befriended so many, most were from London or the surrounding areas. There were some right characters, socials were held at each other's caravans and they all had drinks, food, laughter and dancing in common.

All us kids used to meet up and we'd walk all the way to West Sands, which was a few miles away by the beach. The fun fair was there too, so we'd badger our parents for money to go on the rides and the amusements. Sometimes we would walk all the way along the beach to Pontins, where they had paddle boats.

We also had many friends in Selsey village, whom we used to visit. So, there was always plenty to do.

I think my mum and dad hated the thought of going home, facing reality again. He certainly worked hard enough to merit a break. It was the usual ritual, we'd pack the clothes onto the car, disconnect the gas bottle and put it in the van. Hoover the van out, lock all the windows and close the curtains, all before setting off into town where we would have our dinner before the 90-minute drive home.

The Riviera Restaurant was our favourite choice and it was normally packed, still is to this day (although now called the Boulevard). The meals in there were huge and I'd regularly have the roast chicken, or the cod and chips. To be fair, they had a wide variety on the menu, even to cater for a fussy git like me. I'd even try to make a space for a chocolate nut Sunday, my sister would have a knickerbocker glory, my brother would have a Pingu ice cream.

So, spending at the caravan was very high, it couldn't have been cheap paying for all those rounds of drinks and such! Even though my ma used to coin it in on the fruit machine a few times. The amount of times you'd hear her shout "Woohoo!", followed by the sounds of 'ker clink, ker cling, ker clink' as the fifty pence pieces were paid out into the coin drawer. The money was gathered onto the tin drinks trays to be changed up at the bar! Then mum would finally get a round in (Laughing out loud!!!), even though my dad gave her the money to play the fruit machine in the first place. Bless him.

If we timed it right, we would ask for some money to go next door to the amusements or get a coke float, for we'd have our own place in the 'Harness Room'. It was like a kiddie's disco, where we also played a lot of games. They had a fancy-dress competition once; my sister and I spent the best part of the day making a costume for my little brother. This particular time we made a Rubik's cube costume for him. It looked really good!

When it came to the competition, he decided to go all shy and stubborn, poking his head inside the cube like a tortoise. The compere did everything he could to coax my brother out and introduce himself, but he wasn't having a bean of it! He thought people were laughing in ridicule at him! The compere even poked his microphone down inside the costume.

"I'm not coming out!" my brother ranted.

Despite his ranting, he ended up winning the competition!

The prizes were quite good as well, but more so it was fun and kept us occupied.

One time I even remember dressing up as a scarecrow! They also did a 'Holiday Princess' competition which my sister won, she is beautiful though and my mum and dad were very proud parents. She was a great dancer too and would end up winning the disco dancing competitions. I tried to copy her, but she would totally outshine me.

We took part in a lot of activities and became well known for it. I used to enter into talent competitions, often doing impressions and end up singing 'You'll Never Walk Alone'. I would see my dad in the crowd grinning, my mum waving her arms in the air to my 'Gerry and the Pacemakers' rendition.

Normally I'd finish my routine and then be met by a big round of applause, all apart from one particular year. I came down to the Embassy Bar in west Sands one night; I was up at the bar having a few pints! Obviously, it was a good few years later on and I was allowed to drink alcohol. I was on about my fifth pint, when I was approached by the compere who stated that he was short of entries the talent competition, so would I be interested in making up the numbers?

This is where I differed from my dad, I loved an audience, whereas he would shy away from them. So, I agreed to help out, despite feeling a little tipsy. I used to have a routine where my script centred around the subject of TV shoes and this was the stencil for my act.

I was introduced onto the stage by the compere and was met with a warm round of applause by the audience. As I encroached onto the stage, I stumbled on the cable of the microphone, which lead to some laughter from the audience. I think they thought it was deliberate, resembling the great Freddie Starr, as that was one of his trademarks.

A good audience tonight, I thought to myself. I really used to get a buzz from being up on the stage, often spotting my dad grinning away as usual as I started my routine. Whilst I rattled off my impressions, I would scour the audience for someone to pick on whilst doing my David Bellamy impression. This particular night, I noticed a man with curly hair in the crowd, so I approached him off the stage and started to go through my routine as David Bellamy, who was most famous for his nature documentary hosting and the huge enthusiasm he brought to his programmes, all with a trademark speech impediment.

"Well, gwapple my gwapefwuits! Here we are in the undergwowth, and here is a humped back monkey! And would you like to stand up for the audience?" With that, the gentleman stood up and appeared to have a hunchback!

"Are you happy now!?" he snapped?

The audience gave out a gasp.

Oh my God, I wanted the ground to swallow me up, doing everything I could to revive the act, but the damage had been done.

It was purely unintentional, but it went down like a lead balloon.

I even sang my lungs out, but the crowd's reaction wasn't the best.

Personal note to self, no more David Bellamy Impressions!

That wasn't the last time where I acted the clown.

We used to have celebrity cabaret acts in Selsey too. One day, Lenny Henry did a bit of stand up there and

I threw a packet of square crisps onto the stage to him. He handled it well, he picked them up off the floor and laughed!

"It's weird!" he said, laughing again.

My reason for doing this, is that he was in an advert for Square crisps.

One of the most memorable times I got up on stage, I used to raise money for the 'St Heliers Hospital, CT Scanner Appeal) and I would do a robotic dance to Michael Jackson's 'Beat it'. I did this on numerous occasions and my Moonwalk went down very well with the audience. I raised quite a sum of money and was honoured to be invited to dinner by the late great Sir Harry Secombe, as he was the patron for the charity.

So, as you can see, I was very much the extrovert, in total contrast to my father.

It was fantastic being down in Selsey for the whole of the Summer Holidays, it seemed endless and every day was so different. There used to be a big market near the Windmill, not far from Patrick Moore's house. We'd get a lot of our meat from that market and maybe, if we were luck, we'd be able to pick up a toy. The meat stall was like an auction, definitely reminiscent of Del Boy's way of selling out his suitcase! The meat was delicious though and we'd get steak, barbecue packs and such, plenty for your money too!

I was allowed to buy a stunt kite there once, this kite was bigger than me! I clearly remember being pulled off of my feet many a time and because of that, I wasn't allowed to fly it on my own, especially considering the dangers of the local power lines in the area! I can still recall my dad pulling me back to the ground as I'd get lifted over a meter off of the floor. This was exhilarating, yet sometimes frightening and nearly always exhausting, pulling at the controls to gain height or pull on one side to make it dive, then pull the other side to make it climb again.

I think it's fair to say that I got pretty good with it! The kite had a long ribbon tail, resembling a giant blue sting ray in the sky! That's one thing you could rely on Selsey with, it was usually quite windy! Yet it's weather would differ from inland weather, as geographically it was like a split that was around eight miles out to seat. So, you could have a cloudless sky until you reached Chichester, then the clouds would start forming.

We'd come back from our summer holidays, looking like we'd been abroad to a hot Country! I'd often get a tan whilst flying my kite, or my dad used to put me on horses found in nearby fields. Just simple things in life that provided such happy memories for me. I think my dad enjoyed it too, he even tried roller skating once, trying on my sister's skates and started swinging his arms side to side to gain momentum like a speed skater, then he tried to spin around, only to fall onto his backside!!

Another thing we would do before heading back home, was stopping off at the Shellfish hut at East Beach and get fresh crab and prawns. There was a little duck pond there too, which I used to fish. It's prohibited to fish there now, an oasis for a variety of waterbirds and has carp in it now. Back then, it was just mainly roach and rudd. I remember another kid hooking a duck once, probably the reason why fishing there was eventually stopped! I managed to secure the duck and remove the hook, before taking it back to our caravan. My mum went mad when she heard it quacking in the shower and the mess that it made.

I was always bringing back injured animals. I brought in a crow once, which made my deeply superstitious mum go off the scale as she thought that crows symbolized evil! The poor bird nearly fell off of my arm when she screamed "That that out!". She wasn't so bad about the duck, and funny as it may seem, the duck used to come back to our caravan every year and visit us with her young. It amazed me how she knew which van was ours and there were thousands on the site. Where dis he nest?

I had baby blue tits flying around in the van. I even hatched out a moorhens egg, got told off when I brought in a hedgehog and placed it onto the table. It had a flea circus on it's back! I even brought a tiny bunny back, that had been attacked by a weasel near the archery field when I was sitting fishing, hidden in the tall grass. Amazing to watch such a tiny hunter take down something twice it's size. Yep, I was a proper Doctor Dolittle!

Our last stop would be to Comptons Farm Shop, where we would get all of our vegetables for a roast back at home. Occasionally, we would stop near Ockley on an apple farm and get some Cox's apples. It was considerably cheaper shopping this way and less hassle and stress too! Mum would get salad stuff to go with the crab and prawns.

If it wasn't too late in the day, we'd stop in a pub on the way home. Sometimes the 'White Swan' at Pulborough, or even the 'Old Schoolmaster' near Bury. We'd get a lemonade and a packet of crisps, Mum would have her usual lager, dad would normally have a coke.

Sometimes on the way home, we'd see the police doing spot checks at various lay bys on the route home. My dad sometimes pulled over and made out he was looking under the bonnet and wait for them to go, or wait until they pulled over someone else before leaving the scene himself. He even turned his car around once, going back the way we had come, before an alternative route! We always thought that it was because something was amiss with the car, but it turned out he only had a provisional driving license up until my sister passed her driving test at the age of 18. All those years, without a full license! I could see my mum said that she didn't really know who dad was sometimes! And to think he should go on about what was the right things to do to us, car maintenance, insurance and such.

I think he must have used his dad's license back in the early days, obviously they never had the technology back then to discover the truth! Records were not immediately to hand like they are now. We knew we were nearly home when we reached Dorking, back to reality for a while. The disappointment would show on all of our faces at some point, especially after the summer holidays ended. The traffic used to be dire, we'd come home after the August bank holiday weekend.

Selsey used to have a visiting fun fair during the August Bank Holiday weekend, which was great! It was the last time that all us kids used to congregate together until next Spring time, so we'd meet up with the villagers and make the most of the previous time we had left. It was there I realized my lack of affection for dizzy rides, like the octopus and the Walters, they used to make me sick. The last ride I went on like that was the 'Tunnel of Death' at Carshalton Carnival, where I was sick. My girlfriend Tara found it very amusing! I didn't, however.

Lorraine and Kevin would sometimes fall asleep on the way home, but I was never one to take a nap, even to this day I find it hard and I envoy those who can sleep on a six pence.

So, as you can see, these were very happy times, obviously when Kevin came along, Lorraine and I could re-live some of the childhood memories through his experiences there. For we had our caravan for years, well over two decades in fact. We sadly had to give up our pitch, as it was deemed by the owners that our caravan was too old to stay there my dad fought hard to try and keep it there, but to no avail. He certainly wasn't in a position to another caravan, let alone pay the ground rent each year on top of that. I don't know what happened to our caravan, we still go back there from time to time, to rekindle special memories that we have there.

Going back to the beaches, takes me back to when I used to scour the Groynes and rock pools for crabs and fish. Some things have changed there, but for the most part, it is still relatively untouched. The campsite is now run by an American company, as Bunn Leisure were bought out. It has been modernized somewhat, the Rivier Restaurant is still there under the guise of 'The Boulevard' and there is still a fun fair on the campsite, still going and run by the son of Gary, the owner from when we were kids.

To think that our caravan survived the tornado that struck Selsey many years ago is amazing, for some of the rides were ripped out of the fun fair and thrown into the sea along with a multitude of caravans. It just missed Patrick Moore's house too! We were so lucky to find that our caravan was undamaged. I remember when our parents drove down there to find out what state our caravan would be in, but she was a tough old girl. I still prefer to visit the untouched parts of Selsey to reflect on how lucky we were and truly thankful to my mum and dad for trying to compensate for our sad times in childhood. Now they are both gone too, makes it all the more important to frequent all the old haunts.

They never got another caravan or hired one since they had to give up D13. I think it was too painful for them. They did eventually find another haven to visit, somewhat more affordable too! Going back to Italy, I think was too painful memories for my ma, as we went there a couple of times prior to losing Gillian.

We heard about a place in Spain, south of Alicante, called Denia, which is near Torrevieja. My mum, dad, brother and I flew to Spain, to Alicante, hired a card and headed south towards Denia. Lorraine was now old enough to stay behind if she wished, so she did not join us.

It was an adventure from the start! My dad would be like a kid again and my brother and I absolutely loved it! I can still picture him grinning away, as he'd be getting in touch with his mischievous side. He would start pandemonium by randomly tooting his horn when he was in standstill traffic at a set of lights, starting off everyone else around us, which resulted in chaotic tooting from all the cars! He used to laugh his head off! Or he would shake drivers' hands in the oncoming traffic, who were manually signalling to turn.

"How do you do?!" he'd say, normally to be met by a bemused and confused driver. It amazed me thinking back, how he'd manage to find his way around sod easily. I don't ever remember getting lost, and back then, there was no Sat Nav or Google to rely on. Maybe it was the fact that there were less roads?

That particular holiday we even went to Benidorm and went to the water park close by. I found a joke shop, where I remember buying peppered sugared almonds and far powder. I used to love playing tricks on my grandad, I guess I took after my dad for it. I'd offer to my grandad a tea, and would slip the fart powder into it. don't know whether it was effective or not, as he used to fart a lot anyway!

The water park was memorable too, as I can still envisage thundering down the chute of the kamikaze water slide, it was nigh on vertical at the start of the run, a truly exciting ride that would test your mettle and of course, how well your swimming costume was on as it would take a battering. Even my dad would have a go, sadly my Ma suffered a fall a few years back and she was not able to participate due to a bad back. It was funny to see my dad on the Kamikaze, he'd assume the position he did when he took off on the airplane, where he hated the take-off, during which he'd close his eyes to reveal his 'crow's feet' and tuck in his chin. He was ok with the landing, whereas my Mum hated the landing and would normally squeeze the life out of my hand.

He loved the water, at the hotel swimming pool, there was a wall in the middle of the pool that separated the adult pool from the kiddie's pool. We would both climb onto the wall and attempt to knock each other off. I can still see him gritting his teeth, normally I'd win because I had better balance than him, as long as I could avoid him grabbing hold of me.

We stayed at a nice complex in Denia; however, we did have a couple of run-ins with local residents who exhibited some very anti sociable behaviour. It was a group of lads around my age, who were causing trouble around the pool. I wouldn't let anything happen to my little brother, he is eight years younger than me, so I'd protect. The Spanish kids were putting sea urchins and other things at the bottom of the pool, terrorising some of the others who were using it. I remember one day in particular, where it properly kicked off with them.

We were on sunbeds next to their veranda, when one of the boys started to spit at me from the balcony. That's one thing I really cannot stand and didn't notice at first, until my dad gave me a heads-up.

"Stop fucking spitting at me, you prick!" I shouted up.

They just kept laughing and talking in Spanish, which I didn't understand.

So, I gestured for them to come down, I wanted to do it the English way!

My dad started gesturing to them like a chicken, flapping his arms and shouting "Pollo, pollo!" which is Chicken in Spanish, which is amusing as he didn't speak much of the language either!

They still didn't come down, so he booked their Piaggio into a ditch.

We didn't see them again funnily enough; the pool was now a safer and civil place to reside.

Although we did end up throwing the eggs at their window shutters on the last day after we departed from the villa for the final time!

The other most memorable thing I remember from that particular holiday, was when we were driving back to Alicante airport. Nobody told my dad that it was mandatory to wear a seat belt on the highways. So, we were pulled over by the police in our hire car (dad felt that they profiled tourists, as the hire cars had slightly different number plates to domestic cars).

I felt very anxious at it looked like the policeman meant business, plus they were carrying weapons.

That didn't stop my mum, she was doing her absolute nut in the car and swearing at the policemen, as they levied a penalty charge against us along with an official notice. I think the policeman understood English perfectly well, probably one of the reasons why he wrote out so many tickets. I remember one fine was due to the car not having the registration number etched into the glass of the window of the car.

I remember my dad telling my mum to calm down, as it wasn't helping his cause. Nor did it when my brother laughed as the policeman banged his head whilst peering in through the window to inspect the occupants of the car, the policeman was not amused!

We eventually were allowed to carry on our journey and I think the only thing he never got a ticket for, was speeding.

My dad was quite good like that! His fines totalled well over a few hundred pesetas. I think he ended up getting most of it back by contacting the British consulate. At least he walked away without having been shot!

He was hilarious when we went to Lanzarorte. You used to get 'looky looky' men there trying to sell sunglasses and other little gadgets. He'd call them over and make a ridiculous offer for this that they had to sell.

"My friend, fifteen pesetas!" he'd say!

The 'Looky Looky' just laughed and said "No".

He noticed that my dad had a cigarette lit up.

"Ganja?" one of them asked, thinking it was weed.

"Yeah, ganja!" My dad said.

He handed one of them the lit cigarette, who took a huge drag of it.

"No ganja!" he concluded, smiling.

My dad just laughed.

We saw him a few times over the holiday and I think he enjoyed bumping into us.

I think that was the last holiday that I went to with my parents. I did go on holiday without them when I was twelve years of age, when I was lucky to go on a skiing trip to Austria with my school. My sister went with her too. It must have cost dad a fortune, but he never saw us go without. I went skiing a second time when I moved to grammar school too, and I also went to the Lake District and a field trip to Cornwall. I'm blessed to have been able to go.

I think because of our tragic start in life, he wanted to have happier memories and I know he certainly couldn't have afforded it. He and his brothers went to boarding school and had it a lot tougher, so I think he wanted us to have more than he experienced. I think most parents try to achieve that, I certainly have with my daughter. I cannot life, but we did have bailiffs knock on the door a few times and I'm definitely not ashamed of it either.

Even Christmas we would have a huge mountain of presents, some were kept back for the afternoon. It was a super exciting time in our house. When Kevin was born too, Christmas was relived, even though our beliefs in Santa were minimal by then, it was still a great time in our house.

I could never sleep at the best of times, let alone Christmas! I even saw my dad climbing into the loft through the transom window above my bedroom door, I saw him peering into my bedroom, gritting his teeth as he often did. He saw me peering at him.

"Go to sleep!" he'd bark!

So! That's where our presents were kept! The following year, my sister and I ventured to find them. When we boasted on finding them, our parents deliberately held them back to last to try and put us off the scene, and we ended up getting them in the afternoon.

Our usual ritual for Christmas, was that we had to have a bath and get dressed, then we'd run down into the front room where all the presents were piled up into separate piles. We had to wait to open any of them until wed had breakfast and my Nan and Granddad came up from their house. I'd wait at the passageway window, looking down the alley for them to appear. Unmistakable my grandad was, very tall and my nan was tiny.

The presents were opened once my nana and grandad got settled, normal ritual would be that we took it in turns with opening our presents, reading who they were from. We normally opened the presents from our parents last, or sometimes connecting presents had to be opened in a certain order, so as not to give the game away. I've had some truly memorable presents over the years. 'Simon, which provided many happy hours of fun, computer 'Battleships', 'Operation' and 'Buckaroo'

I even got a big snooker table one year. My dad had to get on the bus with that apparently and he even asked a passerby to keep an eye on it whilst he popped into another shop to get my sisters present. The gentleman declined however; he was overly suspicious as it was at the time of the IRA bombings. Dad got it home eventually; he must have hidden it in the garage I'm guessing as it must have been eight foot long.

They used to play tricks on us too, one year, my sister and all our friends got boot skates. I looked out the passage window, watching them, a bit disappointed that I never got a pair.

"Cheer up! You'd best open this" he said.

I opened the present eagerly, only to find a pair of his work boots in the box.

"Ha! Ha! Very funny!" I said, but I wasn't amused.

"You want this one then" he said, and I opened it to find a pair of boot skates too.

His grins and raising of his eyebrows spoke volumes.

For every year, he managed to make Christmas come true.

I still have some of my action men toys and my sister too has her Sindy. I also found some of my first handheld computer games. We've had to clear out our parents' property, as they have now both sadly passed away and we are in the process of selling the house as I write this.

We'd get presents to open in the afternoon too, normally once dinner had been eaten and everything had been cleared away. After that, the large folding table would be transformed into a casino baize, it would be games time!

We had a horse racing game, where a handle turned and moved a mat backwards and forwards that moved the horses which were placed on it, obviously the first over the line was deemed the winner. We played a card game called 'Newmarket'; this was a game that we could all participate in. Money would be placed in a pot and also on one of the suited king's upward turned in the centre of the table. The idea was to lay the queen down and you would win the money on the king of the corresponding suit.

The person that won the kitty had to get rid of all of their card. So, you'd start with lowest red. The dealer had the choice of two hands, so the other cards in the hand were dead. So, if you had the tow of diamonds for instance, somebody had to lay the three and so on until no-one could go. Then lowest black had to be laid. My nan was murder at it, she was so slow!

"Wait a minute, wait a minute" she'd say.

She'd be heckled by us all, normally by a 'tutting' from my grandad as usual, but she'd normally win which was the funny thing.

"Come to nanny!" she'd say.

I'd sink my face into my hands.

Then normally after, it would be time for dominoes, or brag, or poker. I learned to play many card games, but when I was younger, I was only allowed to spectate. I'd peer over my dad's shoulder or my grandad. My Uncle David would never let me see his cards, just as well really, because sometimes I'd give the game away with an "Ooooooh" or an "aaaaah".

"BJ, shush!" my dad would say. Or my Granddad would say "Onlookers keep quiet!".

I felt so grown up when I was finally allowed to sit in on the game. I'd get told off by my grandad for laying cards out of turn. I got taught how to play cribbage and partnered up with my dad against my Uncle David and my grandad. We were pretty good as a pair. There were lots of laughs, although we all took it very seriously. My dad was very hard to read, he'd usually had his usual tongue hanging out whilst his eyebrows raised, but it was never a 'tell'.

My grandad would normally call the last game. I always wished time never slipped away, as quick as what it did. I certainly miss those days. I haven't played cards in a while. I've had the odd game of dominoes against my partner Tara, she is a great player I must say. Not only does she get dealt a good hand of domines, she can certainly play! Good job it wasn't for money, she would have the shirt off my back.

I've always thanked my mum and dad for a wonderful Christmas. We know how hard they tried to make our Christmas the best and they truly were. The funny thing was, we never asked for anything, yet we always got exactly what we would have wished for. My dad would even get my Mum something she wanted. Something I've always found hard to do. He would never let on to us either, what he had bought for her. I could keep a secret, but Lorraine was terrible for letting the cat out of the bag. Even when dad used to give her hush money, because she'd see him going in or out of the bookies, she'd giggle in front of mum. When she asked why she was laughing, she would grass him up. Poor dad!

As I mentioned earlier, my ma suffered with bouts of depression, she pined for Gillian when she was sadly taken from us at such an early age. She sadly died at only two years of age in April 1974. She unintentionally neglected my sister and I.

Unfortunately, my dad had a vasectomy prior to losing Gillian, as they had three children before the tragedy. I think it was the final straw for my dad when my ma tried to overdose on her Valium and my sister Lorraine and I found her. We would never have wished to be in her shoes. Valium was very addictive and has been proven to do more harm than good, hence why it was eventually banned and had ceased to be given to people. Its high addiction became a massive battle for my mum to kick the habit. I think my dad would have wished he could cease working in order to look after my mum, but that was not possible because he had to keep a roof over our heads.

I am not exactly sure when, but it came to light that it was possible to have a game-changing reverse vasectomy operation. I think because of the circumstance; my mum and dad were at the forefront of this new founded treatment. That must have been hard in itself for my dad to literally put his balls on the table. I am guessing it must have been around 1976, as my brother was born 1977. Back then, obviously the technology was not like today, with keyhole surgery and other instruments that makes the surgery such a swift and successful process.

I can still see my dad walking around in pyjamas, rather gingerly and wincing; this is a very distinctive memory because he never wore pyjamas normally and would usually just go to bed in his pants!

Everything changed in our houseful after this, as it became very obvious that ma was pregnant! It was likely someone had flicked a switch in my mother, her motherly instincts rebooted and she was able to abstain from the Valium that had previously thrown a dark cloud over her life. I don't think I'd have been able to go through that pain that my dad suffered from the reversal!

It became increasingly very real for us as mum's pregnancy went on, excitement heightened for us, Lorraine and I were really excited that we'd be getting a brother or sister. Just to see my mum smile was more than we could ask for. Feeling mum's tummy for kicks of seeing the baby turn in her tummy was magical, it gave us our mum back. There were no disillusions of storks bringing the baby and dropping it down the chimney, for we knew and could see exactly what was happening!

ma had a home delivery and her midwife was amazing and lovely; October 1977 was a very historic time, not only for us as a family, but also for medical history. For my brother Kevin, as he was named, was the first successful baby born due to a reversal! He was deemed a miracle baby and was such a sweet little present, a bundle of joy. He seemed to grin with being content, although it was probably just wind! Our house then became busy with many photographers, the newspapers carried headlines of a miracle baby! He certainly was!

My dad must have been so proud, relieved and probably thought, "wow! I'm going to need a raise with one more mouth to feed!". Kevin became nationally famous for being the first reversal ever. My mum's Auntie in Australia even heard the good news! It definitely was a major turning point for us all. He had a family shield around him as he was so special to us all. I even got to help bath him and care for him, as did my sister too. Noone was going to hurt him.

We used to take him out when he was old enough at the caravan; I used to tease him occasionally on the whole, it was very much enjoyable. Our neighbours a few doors down at home became his Godparents, as they were unable to have children, sadly. Lorraine and I would tease him and he'd run up to their house and he'd come back down with a big bag of sweet! He got absolutely spoilt rotten by Joe and Joan.

He then got to an age where mum could go back to work. In her early days before she had us, she used to work on the tills in a shop. After Kevin had grown up sufficiently, she took job at a children's nursery, where she had a very serious fall whilst at work, resulting in a very serious injury to her back. Just when things started to get better for us, the family were once again back in very tough times. Some days mum was completely bed bound, which had various knock-on effects. She eventually had an operation on her back and I remember going to visit her in hospital. It must have been so hard for my dad, although he tried, his culinary skills were very limited; it became a long-standing joke about his bouncing burgers and lumpy, soggy mash potatoes! He could cook eggs, but that's sadly about all he could cook! It must have been a continuous nightmare for my parents.

I'll never forget the day when I saw my dad act like a hero again, he acted so calmly. I remember being at the sink washing up for a change for my mother. A rarity back then, I can tell you! All of a sudden, we heard a few bit bangs! It sounded like thunder, but only louder. Then I saw a big mushroom cloud, situated over the next square in the residential estate that we lived in.

My dad came out of the living room, and I shouted "Quick, somethings happened! Together we ran up the alley way towards the cloud of smoke. A crowd had already gathered outside. "What are you all standing here for, there could be someone inside!?" I cried. I went to try and get in to the house via a porch window, when my dad stopped me. "BJ, let's go around the back!".

So, we rushed down the alley to the back garden gate, he opened the back door to the front room. Smoke billowed out of the door, followed by a man who looked very dazed and sported a singed beard. After that the man we knew owned the house emerged, followed by his son. As we entered into the smoke-filled room, the curtains caught alight from the oxygen that rushed in from the open door. The bearded man came back in equipped with a hose. I think the shock clouded his judgement as he started to spray the water dangerously close to the television, which was still on. My dad grabbed it off of him and slapped him "Pull yourself together, you'll kill us all!" he said. My dad grabbed the curtains and put them out with his hands.

"Wookie is here! Where is he!?" shouted someone. Wookie was a very large Weimaraner, who had shot upstairs and hid apparently. I tried to retrieve him, but I ended up falling over the side of the stairs. He was eventually found after the fire brigade and the bomb squad turned up! It turned out that the owner was preparing detonators for a firework display, when statis from the carpet set off one of the detonators, which resulted in a chain reaction, hence the series of bangs and explosions! Thankfully nobody was seriously hurt, the house owner's son had a bad burn on his thumb.

It could all have been so much worse had it not been for the quick thinking of my dad; looking back, I can't believe he had taken that experience so well, considering the trauma he had suffered in the past. He suffered post-traumatic stress disorder from our fire when we were kids, where he would run around the bedroom, shouting and tried to climb out of the bedroom window a number of times like he did on that fateful day. I used to hear my mum shout at him to get back into bed. It used to scare the hell out of me!

Sometimes he'd sleepwalk to our bedrooms and just open the door and stand in the doorway. "Dad" I'd whisper, only to be met with silence. I also had occasional nightmares too, which is why I slept with the light on. Back then opportunities for counselling were unheard of; now our scars are deep and the damage has been done. Each of us developing defence mechanisms and still suffering with various triggers, such as hearing a fire engine, which used to set me off into a panic.

I began to understand what my dad had gone through and was still experiencing. The bond between him and myself became ever stronger, he also looked on me as a young man then and dare I say it, like his best mate. For he was certainly mine, that bond got stronger than every back in 2001, which a random event resulted in me coming to relieve by dad's tragic footsteps on the night GIllian was taken away from us all.

I still can't believe the events of this particular day, things certainly happen for a reason! That day, I had gone fishing with my buddy Simon, to Tunbridge Wells. We were both very dedicated fisherman and went in all weathers. We used to take turns in driving, that day, it was my turn to drive. In the past, we would have sat all day without a bite. On this particular day, we both decided to call it a day and I still do not know why, as it was contrary to our usual behaviour of staying until the last possible minute for a fish.

Simon had a fish and I had one bite, so it wasn't the best of days! So, we packed up and headed back to Wellingtonia Way in Edenbridge, which is where Simon lived. Wellingtonia way was a cul-de-sac and I remember thinking that it was similar in appearance to the one In the television series 'Brookside', with terraced housing side by side.

I got out the car, went around and opened up the boot. It was then that I smelt the smoke, which immediately set off my triggers, for I knew it was not a bonfire, but something was wrong. Having previous first-hand experience, I knew there was a house fire nearby. In addition to the smell of smoke, I could hear a smoke alarm. Sure enough, there was a plume of smoke coming from the rear of one of the rows of houses, so I investigated further.

I jumped over a garden fence adjacent to the houses, looked up and noticed a tower of flames from one of the top windows. My worst fears had been met, yet again! I jumped back over the fence and shouted to onlooking neighbours who were outside their houses, not knowing there was a problem. "Quick, call the fire brigade, there's a fire! Which house is it coming from?" I shouted, to the crowd.

A neighbour showed me where it may have been coming from. There was a row of four doors, so in turn I opened the door letterboxes until one suddenly billowed out smoke from it. One of the neighbours and I then proceeded to kick the door in, which eventually flew open and we were met with a wall of smoke! It was an upstairs dwelling from a downstairs doorway.

"There's no point all of us going in, I'll go in and you wait here" I said to the neighbour. I crawled on all fours, up the stairs, the smoke was right down to the floor. I shouted for a torch, as it was like a black cloak had been thrown over me. At the top of the stairs, I was met with a locked child gate, which I eventually unbolted, before then hearing a woman screaming and banging on the door to my left. It turned out to be the bathroom she was locked in; I shouted to her that we were in her flat and she was frantic. I could hear kids crying!

"How many kids have you got?" I shouted.

Suddenly, I was handed a torch.

"I'm going in!" I said.

So, I started crawling as low as I could, it was quite scary as I could not see a thing, but only could hear the fire. The smoke was drying out my throat; I used my Gore-Tex fishing jacket as a filter to try and breathe. Even though I had a very powerful lamp, the smoke was still blocking its beam. As I crawled a little further, I saw what I thought were a pair of luminous trainers, it turned out to be the socks of little Ben, one of the children!

I dropped the torch and picked Ben up, before shouting out that I'd managed to find one of the children. I gingerly moved towards the shouting of the neighbours at the top of the stairs. I shielded Ben as I went back down the stairs, keeping my back to the wall. As I came out of the house, I passed Ben over to the neighbours, regained my breath and entered back into the house. By now the smoke seemed thicker than ever, I couldn't even see where the lamp laid, but somehow, I stumbled across it. I had no idea what direction I was crawling, I was running out of breath. I suddenly laid there thinking that I was going to die.

I started to think to myself, "You've gone and done it now!" and I was praying that the fire brigade would come soon. I was thinking about my beautiful daughter, Georgia, who was only five years old. I had the realization, that I was never going to see her or my family again. Breathing through my jacket seemed less effective now. This was it, I thought!

Then suddenly, I heard a baby cry for their Mum. That was close! I reached out and suddenly felt two baby feet, it was Charlie!" She was strapped in her car seat on the sofa. It was like an imaginary hand had picked me up from the floor and I got a second wind. I picked up the whole car seat, and shouted that I'd got another one. I wasn't going to waste time trying to undo the car seat in these conditions. I was bad enough in broad daylight.

I was screaming "Where are you?" and I kept my back to the wall. I tried to stay aware of my direction, but it was still difficult to gear my bearings. It seemed like eternity; I can tell you. I handed over Charlie to a neighbour, but I knew we weren't out of the woods. Poor Sonya was still locked inside the house. What must have been going through her mind?

I shouted to her through the door that we had her kids. I tried frantically to break down the door to get to her, I was measuring paces to the door to try and break it down. The neighbours were amazing that made it all possible for me to do what I did and to be able to tell the tale. Suddenly we were handed two hand axes, so we frantically started hacking through the door. Heaven knows how we weren't hitting each other. The door started to fragment, suddenly there was a shout from one of the neighbours that the fire brigade had arrived. I really can't tell you how relieved I was to hear that.

I came back outside and dropped to the floor outside on all fours, coughing and retching. I was filled with so many emotions. The firemen finally freed Sonya and she was reunited with her kids. She was very emotional, quite rightly so! She gave me a big hug, which triggered off my emotions.

One of the firemen turned out to be one of Simon's good mates, who was at his wedding and I had met him before when we had played paintball for Simon's stag do.

I used to work part time at the paint ball site and I shot the hell out of him in one of the games called the Stag Hunt. I didn't recognize him at first, he addressed me by my nickname, which is 'Harry' or 'Aitch' (due to my surname).

"It's me Aitch, you shout the hell out of me, remember?!" he said. "How the hell did you find you way about? We had breathing apparatus on and it was very difficult?" he asked.

"I don't know mate" I replied.

The ambulance crew insisted that I went to hospital to get checked over, due to the severity of my smoke inhalation. No again! They were taking me back to Tunbridge Wells, where we had just come from. To be honest, I just wanted to go home. I looked like a chimney sweet and smelt just how I remember when we had our house fire. I'd already called home and contacted my Mum and Dad, and technically explained what had happened.

Mum, dad and Kevin drove to Tunbridge Wells to get me. I got a massive hug from my ma, my dad patted me on the head, raised his eyebrows and smiled through gritted teeth. That was the nearest I got to a hug. We went to a nearby pub, where I explained what happened and a few tears were shed. I just wanted to go home now, and see my partner and my daughter, who is my reason for living.

When I got home, I received the biggest hug even from my partner. The realization started to overshadow my shock. It felt like I was cursed, being forever tormented by the horror of fires. I immediately took off my clothes to be washed and sat in the bath numb and dumbfounded. My hair felt like straw from the soot and it took ages to get my face clean. My fishing jacket had to be washed a number of times to try and get rid of the awful smell of smoke. The trauma from the experience was enough to give me grey hair within days, so that was my third occasion experiencing the horror of fire.

When I woke up the next morning, I was visited by newspaper reports. The fire was ironically around the time that my sister passed away, which made it even more difficult to process. Then I was doubly taken back when I received a bottle of champagne from Piers Morgan.

I was also informed that I had been nominated for a Pride of Britain award, for 'Outstanding Acts of Bravery'. It was a great honour to receive such an accolade, I just did what I could and I would not have achieved this if it hadn't been for the neighbours. The post trauma I suffered is easing over the years, I try to self-counsel myself to lift me out of the negative emotions that I got. I no longer suffer with nightmares or waking up in sweats.

I really understood part of how my dad felt.

It was a massive buzz for my family, going to the televised Pride of Britain awards. I only agreed to take part on the condition that my whole family would be permitted to attend the ceremony. My daughter who was five at the time, was super excited as she was told that Robbie Williams was going to be at the awards. I was super nervous, I know that! I didn't even have anything to wear until Ollie Picton Jones very kindly got me a beautiful suit and clothes to wear.

The biggest thing I got from all this, was that I realized just how proud my mum and dad were of me. Lots of my friends contacted me when the story was edited in the National newspapers; I also did a reconstruction of the event for the series '999'.

I kept thinking "What am I going to say when I collect my award?". The planned schedule was that we were to travel up to London Park Lane, to the Cumberland Hotel, where were all going to meet the other award winners and the years previous winners. We were meeting Carol Vorderman there and she would introduce us and gave a background of why we were there.

There were some truly inspiration stories from many of the awarded winners, of all ages too! Rachael Edwards put me in mind of my daughter and was in fact the same age as her. It was truly an honour to be sitting at the table with Carol Vorderman, for she was one of my idols. I loved and still do love the TV show 'Countdown', which Carol did the mathematics round on.

I was still thinking of what I was going to say! It wasn't coming!

I was due to appear on breakfast TV in the morning and had a personal assistant, who looked after me. She asked me if I was getting nervous, before reassuring me that I'd be OK and what I did was truly amazing.

I was up early in the morning and I went with my dad. He was grinning as usual. I felt like I was going on a job interview. John Stapleton came in and said hello to me and Donny Osmond was also there. My dad did his usual moment of embarrassment, starstruck by celebrity, he said to Donny that his dad had told him about some of the songs that he'd sung. I rolled my eyes and apologized on dad's behalf. I don't really remember much about that morning, only that I was interviewed by Andrew Castle, but that's about it.

We briefly returned back to the hotel afterwards, before it was time to head off to the Hilton Hotel, which was just the road from The Cumberland. I hadn't ever felt butterflies in my stomach as bad as this before. I remember squeezing my partners hand so tight, we had a champagne reception just before the main event took place. My daughter looked so beautiful, we had bought her a special dress and she was very excited that she was going to see 'Wobbly Williams', as she called him. For a little girl of five, she was very knowing and was to be able to recognize certain stars and celebrities that would turn up for each award.

It was a very surreal day, I had not one glass of champagne on the go a time, but two. We were in one of the posh suites on the first floor, waiting for the filming of the awards to start. I gazed out of the big glass windows overlooking Park Lane and you could see loads of flashes from the press cameras, for the stars that were pulling up outside the hotel. I caught a glimpse of Chris Eubank being lit up by the multitudes of flashes from the cameras.

Eventually, came my time to mingle. My mouth was really dry and my palms were sweaty. Georgia was with me. I told her to be on her best behaviour, which she was anyhow. I remember the first person I talked to was Charlie Dimmock and I asked her when she was going to do my garden! It was my way of ice breaking I think, more so than trying to get my pond built! As I glanced around, I could see many people that even I certainly recognized.

Cilla Black was talking to Des Lynham, former Prime Minister Tony Blair was there too.

I saw Georgia make a beeline for Tamsin Outhwaite, who remarked on how cute she was. I felt like I was dreaming. Suddenly Georgia saw Geri Halliwell. "Geri!" she shouted. She ran over to her and Geri stooped down to greet her, only to be nearly knocked over as Georgia threw herself into her arms. "Georgia!" I bellowed. I totally forgot about where I was momentarily. My loud voice seemed to stop the whole room and all eyes seemed to set on me. It definitely was a reality check!

Eventually the time came for the filming of the award ceremony to start, so we made our way downstairs to the main hall. It was like a Michelin restaurant, beautiful chairs and tables were decorated to the highest degree with sparkling glasses and cutlery. We were guided to our tables, where would find our name tags, indicating where we were to be seated.

I had the greatest of honours and pleasure to be seated with Simon Weston and his wife. My dad looked in his element, he was grinning from ear to ear. "Psst, psst, look, Norman Wisdom!" he said. "Mr Grimsdale!" he blurted out Norman's catchphrase in a higher pitched voice and laughed cheekily, followed by a scowl from my Mum at him. Dad loved Norman! Then dad pointed over to me, to look beside where I was sitting and it was John Barnes, such a nice man. He introduced himself and he sat with Georgia when I had to get up to receive my award. I wish I had more time to talk to some of the celebrities that gave up their time to be at the awards.

I saw Mick Hucknell drift past as I was being interviewed by one of the reporters. I think my partner Tara managed to speak to him. I felt truly honoured when Sir Roger Bannister came over to me, so did Piers Morgan and Mark Spitz. I was like a rabbit caught in headlights!

The order of the day was to be started by a three-course meal. It was a very fancy menu. I myself was a bit of 'plain Jane', but I was super nervous too, which negated my appetite anyhow. I was unusually drawn to the wine that was on the table, it wasn't normally what I would drink, but I needed some sort of Dutch courage! I even drank Simon Weston's quota as he didn't drink.

I think Georgia loved it, as the starter was her favourite, it was salmon! She enjoyed it that much that she ate mine. It was my first time that I had dauphinoise potatoes!

Talking to Simon really put me at ease, as I've never been one for 'papping' celebrities to be honest, but I certainly was in awe to have Simon Weston present me with my award and truly a braver man than myself. He spoke with so much wisdom. Eventually dinner was over and it was time to start recording once the tables were cleared. Now I was getting really nervous!

The buzz of conversation subsided and Carol Vorderman introduced the Pride of Britain Awards. I had heard the basic crux of all the stories, but when they were added to film recreations clips and interviews, it made it more dramatic. At times, I wondered if I deserved to be there to be honest. The more I listened to the stories, the more choked up and emotional I felt. I'd nearly drank the table dry.

I remember Georgia sitting on my lap, squealing with excitement as she saw Robbie Williams come up on the stage to present an award to Rachael Edwards. I know my story would soon be revealed and was holding Tara's hand so tight. I felt like I needed to cry, but I managed to hold it together. I suddenly heard my name being mentioned and then a short film footage of my story was shown. I looked over to my parents, my dad smiled and raised his eyebrows. I think telepathically that was his hug to me and proud look, maybe.

I was introduced by Carol Vorderman and was encouraged to approach the stage to receive my award. John Barnes offered to hold Georgia whilst I approached the stage. My eyes were burning, my heart was nearly jumping out from my chest. I was met by a huge round of applause as I looked into the audience, I saw a few teary eyes. I honestly don't know how I didn't cry. I was deeply honoured to receive my awards from one of the bravest men I know, the other was my father in my eyes, but I knew he would not have appreciated addressing that in front of such a crowd. I think he knew he was my greatest hero.

The room went silent as I was asked to speak. I took a deep breath and I composed myself, I realized that I had made a speech!". "I just need to get my breath, I was asked if I could think of a braver man than myself, there's one standing right next to me." I said, gesturing to Simon Weston with my trembling voice. I also thanked the neighbours for their help that made the rescue possible, and also probably averted me losing my life.

I could see my parents looking proud and applauding me.

I hurried out and went to the toilet, it seeded surreal standing at the urinals alongside Paul Young. When I came out of the toilets, I heard someone call me and it was Vinnie Jones. So, I walked over to him. He remarked on my story and I thanked him and quickly changed the subject and talked about that I'd seen him play football. He asked me if I thought he'd played well and I said "Not really!". He laughed. He was a lovely man and made a fuss of Georgia too.

I'd heard that Robbie Williams had gone into a club/bar underneath the Hilton, so I tried to take Georgia in to meet him, but the doorman would not let her in sadly. At least she saw him.

We did a little more mingling and got a few autographs on the day. It was truly a memorable day for us all, the wards were to be aired the next day. Even though I was grateful for being nominated for the ward, it brought back all the horrors that I had experienced, even watching back the footage, I found very hard. It was also plastered all over the Daily Mirror and other papers too. My story was eventually aired right on the news and I suppose people switched on to watch the news, only to be met by my story.

The phones started ringing and some people hadn't heard that I was nominated for an award; I was given a holiday as well by Sir Richard Branson, as the awards were sponsored by Virgin. Although I was grateful for the holiday, I didn't have a pot to piss in! I would have preferred getting one of the prizes that the kids got, at least I could have sold it! I had been offered money for my story by a certain magazine, but they said I breached my contract with them for the sole rights of the story. So, they declined paying me, sadly. That would have come in handy for the holiday spending money!

It was a wonderful holiday though, I originally was meant to go to the Algarve, but I was unable to make the dates. I rang Virgin up and explained my situation to the lady on the phone. I think she must have thought I was bonkers, or it was a massive wind up! You've been given a holiday by Richard Branson and you can't go? Yeah, right!

I finally did manage to get it rearranged for another date and a different place. We ended up going to Maspalomas in the Gran Canaria, it was here that we met a couple from near Leeds, a wonderful couple that had a little girl the same age as ours. It was a small complex that had its own pool and we just chilled around the poolside. Georgia would play with Niamh and we would sit around the pool with Bernard and Helen. We go on that well that we met up again and were to stay at their house in September of 2001.

I remember that stay very well as England beat Germany 5-1 in the qualifiers for the 2002 World Cup. It was an unforgettable night, beer was free flowing and this 'Southern Softie' had to show that he could drink, it was a brilliant night and we were made very welcome by all the locals. The next day I had a banging head and a hangover from hell. I was taken up the countryside where they filmed the opening credits of 'Heartbeat' but not all of the way, as it was the time of the 'foot and mouth' disease outbreak. The wind was enough to blow my hangover from my sleepy head! A truly memorable time and good friends that had met on the way.

I wish I could say that this was the last fire I have had to experience, but I sadly encountered another!

There wasn't such a happy ending to this episode either, it was the year my dad died too sadly, 2005. Tara and I were on our way to The Epsom Derby and as we approached Rose Hill Roundabout, I noticed the windows blown out in the top flat of one of the houses, the fire was truly raging.

Tara pulled over and I rang 999 and asked for the fire brigade. The operator said that the fire brigade would be about ten minutes away. I explained that they didn't have ten minutes, I gave the address and decided I had to do something. Tara pleaded with me not to go in, but I couldn't just watch.

I ran into the entrance of the flats. There were six flats in total within the building, two ground floor, two first floor and finally two flats on the second floor. I remember banging on the doors as I rushed up and shouted that there was a fire! As I got to the top, I could see the fire glowing at the base of the door. I banged on the door opposite, no answer! So, I banged once again and shouted "Fire!".

Suddenly, the door opened and a young lady was stood there in her dressing gown with her hair in a towel. "You've got to get out, your neighbour has a fire!" I advised her. I heard a bath running and asked her if she had a bucket. She kindly lent me it and I decided I had to get in there to help. The door was fairly easy to kick in. I filled the bucket and went into her flat. It was a proper goer; it was like a horror version of 'It's a knockout!'. The fire had taken a real hold and I ended up burning my hand and dropping the bucket. Suddenly, the fire brigade turned up, so I stepped aside and let them get on with it!

I broke down in tears. Why me, again?! It was like I was being punished. I could not stop crying this time. There was somebody in there too. Due to the nature of where the fire was, they could not treat the casualty they managed to get out of the burning house. They had to treat the person at the top of the stairs, so the young lady had to stay in her flat whilst they were treating the casualty. One of the firefighters was a lady and she consoled me and tried to reassure me that I'd given the person a chance, plus I managed to help avert a major disaster. Once I composed myself, I melted into the crowd. I tried to put it in the back of my mind, but I couldn't. Once I cleaned myself up, we tried to carry on as normal. My friends could not believe it when I told them.

It was still playing on my mind, eventually I found out that the injured man had passed away. I was deeply upset, even though I tried to seek the positives in the outcome and what the female firefighter had said to me.

That was the fourth fire I had been involved in.

I felt like I wanted to go back and mysteriously leave a bucket on the lady's doorstep that I borrowed, but I wanted to stay incognito. The event even made the local papers asking for this mystery man to come forward. I didn't want any recognition for it, it was nice however to hear the young lady was truly thankful and I did get some comfort from this.

I have had one more bad experience since and I sincerely hope it will be my last. I have enough bad memories to haunt me for the rest of my living days, but I have to face it again, I will try to be no different. Please God that I don't!

My family helped me through my struggles, in fact, so did many of my friends. These tend to be the best counsellors by way of giving reason, affection and love. One particular friend of mine, Andy, I met on a building site just after I won my award. He became a good companion and workmate. My Dad, Andy and I went from job to job together. Andy was and still is a great listener, we shared a lot in common and we were of the same age group too. I got to meet lots of new friends through him. They're a great bunch, most loved to party and we'd have great social get togethers. Whether it was football events such as the European Championships or the World Cup qualifiers, or just birthday and other social times.

The horse racing at Epsom Derby was always a good one, where sometimes we would end up back at someone's house as a follow-on. Some used to carry on the whole weekend. I couldn't do that! It amazed me how some could and still function for Monday too.

Andy also shared common ground with my dad too, not many of my mates achieved that. They'd talk about football quite a bit, quite a lot in fact. They both had unbiased views surrounding various teams and players and had good knowledge too. My Dad used to try and get me involved in football more, but I loved my fishing.

They also liked to talk about music, my dad was a big fan of blue beat and reggae and was a mod in his younger days. He'd tell stories of his clubbing days, but it was the football that was his main love. They would analyse the weekend football or talk about up-and-coming players; he had a good eye for future stars of the game! Dad loved Manchester United, we were all United fans in our family. He even went to see 'The Busby Babes' play and George Best was one of his favourites.

He used to go to matches with my brother, I'd go on the odd occasion. It was like he reverted back to his youth, he'd show his impish side from time to time, he'd even try to get away without paying his train fares, as he believed that they really needed to improve their service before he'd start paying!

Sometimes he'd get stopped and he'd show his 'fire safety awareness pass' to the inspectors and say he was railway staff. He used to convince himself as well as others. He even used it one day to get into a football match at Crystal Palace once. The first steward he showed it to said "Nice try mate!", but Dad persisted and went to another entrance and finally succeeded in gaining entry along with my brother.

I remember going to Crystal Palace football ground once when we went to see Manchester United play Wimbledon. Wimbledon were temporarily playing there due to the closure of their stadium at Plough Lane. My Dad had joined the crazy gang membership, as it was a gateway for obtaining tickets for Manchester United matches.

This particular match, my dad noticed that the first aid room was next to the players' lounge where Manchester United were. So, he called over the steward and asked if he could take my brother over to the first aid room as his arm was in a cast and was hurting him. So, the next thing was they got to meet Alex Ferguson and a few of the players, they were both in the element.

It wasn't really my cup of tea as I was like a trouble magnet. I kept to myself when I went, I never wore scarfs or my football shirt and I'd just sit quietly watching the game. I got started on by a bloke, randomly sitting next to me once. I remember it like it was yesterday. I'd gone to Crystal Palace with my dad, we were playing Wimbledon once again.

Eric Cantona had just returned from his band for his Kung Fu kick on a spectator. Some of the decisions from the ref, I thought were a bit unfair and harsh on him, turning to my dad and commented that it was never a foul. The next thing happened, was the man standing next to me growled at me "You Cockney Reds Make me sick; you should be sitting over there with your fans!"

"Shut up you prick and just watch the game!" I snapped at him. I don't think he expected that I think he realized it wasn't good to poke a bear with a stick! I was told by my brother that dad also had a word in his ear when I went for a pint at half time.

I think when we went to see Man United play Tottenham Hotspur at White Hart Lane was the worst experience I endured. Even the eerie walk from the station to the ground was bad enough. We were like prisoners being escorted around by the police. This time we were in the away end and were situated right next to the fence separating us from the home fans. They were more like angry mobs than people coming to watch a match.

A man shouted over to me from the home fans and he asked me to get the attention of the man sitting next to me. "Oi mate, he wants you!" I said and pointed over the guy. As the man next to me looked over, the other man gestured hand slaps to his head shouting "Oi mate, you're bald!" to him. So, the bloke next to me started to offer him out. With that the other man started to try and scale the tall fence to get to him. I mean, really?! What happened to watching the game?

I felt very much out of my comfort zone to be honest. My dad deemed seem fazed by any of the goings on, he was always glued to the game and he'd only react to people blocking his view when standing!

I enjoyed going to Chelsea, as it was a friendlier atmosphere there and the journey there was pretty straight forward. I recall going to a match one day with my brother, my dad and my brother-in-law Paul, who was a Chelsea fan. Kevin, my brother, would always wear his football scarf, hat and a big foam 'United' hand. I never used to wear anything, neither did dad. Kev could only have been around ten or eleven years old at the that time and we went into a pub along the The King's Road for a pre-match pint, the pub was called the Nell Gwynne. As we walked in, we were met by a sea of blue and white, there wasn't one red shirt in there apart from the one worn by Kevin.

I immediately went to the toilet and remember thinking that this was a huge mistake being in there. The

Chelsea fans loudly booed and hissed at Kevin, jeering! "Oh my God, we are gonna get it!" I thought. When I came back out from the toilet the Chelsea fans were chanting to us. My brother had a bit of a gate hole on him and he gave back as good as he got, pointing his big foam finger and danced and sang "We're all part of Fergies Army" back at them. He was met with Laughter, more boos and jeers, but it didn't deter him, he just sang louder. I put my head in my hands.

Typically, Dad wasn't fased as usual. Paul was laughing! A man came over to us and said that took a lot of bottle walking in there and he offered to buy us all a drink! I got to admit, that I was very worried up until this point. Needless to say, we got out of the pub unscathed!

The only unpleasant moment we had at the game was with a mouthy Chelsea fan, who swore at my brother and told him to sit down when he jumped up when we scored. He got put into his place though, not only from us, but from some of the Chelsea fans around us. That's the only bad moment I can ever imagine or remember when we went to Stamford Bridge.

It was Crystal Palace where I used to get problems, my second team, as I was born not far from the ground. One time we were in a pub having a pre-match drink, when a community support officer came into the pub on his patrol. A man not far from me raised his voice and said to the officer "OINK!" and started laughing. The officer mistook me being the person who said it and got into my face. "What did you say?!" he said?

"I never said anything!" I replied.

"Well, that's alright then!". He added.

Sheesh! Talk about being in the wrong place at the wrong time! Here's me just minding my own business! It was times like this that made me think I was glad I was a fisherman. That day did have a funny note though, my dad had a 'Laurel and Hardy' moment when we went into a café to sober him up after he'd very unusually had a lot to drink in the Cherry Tree Pub. Dad slipped down the stairs leading up into the café, as his heels must have been wet as he had and slipped on every step as he was on a slippery slope. My brother and I still laugh about that to this day.

The Final Chapter

We were working away on this particular job; Colchester was too far to commute every day for us. We were now a trio, as opposed to the two of us. Andy decided to join us and we worked together as an effective team. As I mentioned, Andy used to call my dad 'The Guru', he'd normally get the job of doing the mains and we'd take care of the electrics out on field if you like. We'd do the trunking runs and high-level stuff, as my dad had already earned his stripes doing that! He'd just issue a plan and we'd make it happen.

We had got this job through working for the contracts manager on a previous job in Kingston. He knew we were the men for the job. For a general is normally only as good as the men they lead, in my opinion. Our job was to build a temporary store in the car park, adjacent to the original store that was going to be refurbished. The temporary store was like a circus tent. Whilst the tent was being erected, we were disconnecting supplies in the existing store.

I can still see my dad looking over his glasses and looking at the drawing of the plans for construction. It was going to be a tricky install as most of the electrical fixtures were to be supported by a framework of unistrut and wire catenaries. The install had to be carried out in scissor lifts too. Trunking could be made at floor level, as it was all to scale, so this would be my dad's job. His fabrications were amazing! He made making the bends look so easy and enjoyed doing them too! One of the reasons I guess Andy also called him 'The Guru';.

I don't know if I mentioned it previously, but my dad loved a cigarette. He'd often get into trouble for smoking where he was not meant to, I think sometimes it was so habitual to him that he wasn't conscious he was doing it! On this site, there was a foreman who was a non-smoker. There was also a bit of 'North and South' divide on the job, between us and the foreman's operatives. Sometimes I felt like I wanted to put him on the deck due to the way he came across, particularly the way he spoke to my dad.

He asked my dad how many fags he smoked a day at work. My dad, I think, just came up with any figure, he told him he smoked ten. He calculated that was five minutes a fag, which equated to fifty minutes of his time. I would describe the foreman as a proper knob jockey. I think the funniest moment was when he accused us of taking out time with the double sets in the trunking. It was quite a big bit of trunking and there was a lot of measuring and cutting to be done!

The foreman tried to rubbish us and said he'd demonstrate how quick and easy it was to make a double set, only to fuck it up and waste a bit of trunking, and also to be met by jeers and laughter from us three. I think it was at this point he realized that he needed to 'butt out' and mind his own business. Regardless of my dad's cigarette breaks, we were moving along nicely. It did start slow to be fair, but we came up against a problem with static build up from the plastic flooring inside the tent. I still laugh about it now as it was really comical!

It all began when I heard the tent erector scream like a girl and star swearing.

"What's the matter mate?" I asked.

"I keep getting a shock, it fucking hurts!" he said.

"Stop being a tart!" I said and laughed at him.

A few minutes later, he screamed again.

Up until this point, I thought he was making a mountain out of a molehill. But then I had a taste of it myself and I got close to the studs, when suddenly I got a massive static shock as it discharged.

I too screamed and the tent erector laughed.

"See! Hurts, don't it?!" he said.

"Right, everyone out of the tent!" I shouted.

So, we put fly-leads off the floor to the steels to reduce the static charge.

It was so severe, it was like a cattle prod or a stun gun.

Now it was safe to work on.

As I mentioned earlier, because Colchester was a mission to travel to on a daily basis, we decided to stay in a bed and breakfast during the week and travel home on the Friday. We found a fantastic bed and breakfast called 'The Four Sevens', the lady who ran it mothered us all. It was very homely, well-kept and she cooked an amazing breakfast too! She also put up with Andy and myself breaking some of her house rules too, as we'd often come back late after going into town for a cheeky pint or two. It was funny one night; we had ventured up into the town to get something to eat when this mahoosive man who seemed like he was not all the ticket started to follow and shadow my dad. The man continued to follow him all the way along Crouch Street. Andy noticed my dad reach into his pocket and pull out his keys and put them in between his fingers. As I mentioned that his nickname was Butchy because he was growing up. He went to a boarding school and had a rough life so anything went with him as part of survival. It was at this point that he turned to face the man following him. The man realised that my dad was going to take action if he did not back off. Andy just laughed. He still remembers that incident to this day. There were other incidents similar to this we as a three experienced on other jobs.

It was here that I noticed something was wrong with my dad. As I mentioned before, he was rarely sick and he never moaned when he hurt himself, but I noticed him wincing with pain and getting up in the hours of night to have a bath. I asked him if he was OK and he'd just shrug it off and say he was fine.

The intensity of the pain got worse and became more frequent. Despite this, he carried on working. I think he tried to hide it from me, not that I think I could do much about it. He still kept a brave face and we managed to complete the job successfully. He still had time to joke, as he used to wind the Northerners up.

We had a 'North against the South' night where we played various games like darts, which all started when Kevin the Contracts Manager said he'd take us all out for a drink when we completed the job. Believe it or not, his idea of a drink was by way of a tea or coffee which he got slated for and we called him a tight Northerner! That's how it all came about of the challenge and yes, we did win everything and yes, he did buy a few drinks too. It was a great night!

dad's pain was getting worse, something had to be done. It was decided that he would have a scan in Turkey when he was going on holiday with my ma. To have one in the UK proved to be too expensive via private Healthcare and there was a great waiting list to have one on the NHS. A bit disgraceful really, when you think that you pay all this National Insurance and taxes for diddly squat. We were hoping the Sun was going to help his back, but little did we know what was ahead of us.

He managed to get a scan done, which cost around a hundred and fifty pounds. The only down side was that the report was in Turkish. So, we needed to get it translated and once that was done, it was very apparent what dad had.

We managed to get a hospital appointment for dad and the results of the scan were given to the NHS to help move things along. I can still remember the name of the doctor to this day and the pain and sadness that I feel is just the same as it was then, that I feel too date.

He came into a room which we were all gathered in and told us that dad had Metastatic Adenocarcinoma, which was a cancer that cure for, said sorry and then left the room. The expression on his face, I will never forget. ma started to cry. This was it? No explanation? Surely it was a mistake? Nothing they can do?

It would have been nice to have answers or to be left down more gently, I hope I'm told in a better way when I'm dying. We got a lot of answers from research that we undertook ourselves. I still was in denial and kept kidding myself that there had to be something we could do.

You could see the sadness in his eyes, he did not comment on it though. I felt I could look at him and I knew what he was thinking, more so on how he felt. I think he must have felt angry he was going to be cheated of his life. I think he felt cheated not to be able to watch his grandchildren grow up. A majority of his life seemed to be filled with pain and misery, he certainly deserved to see happier days.

I think I cried for him; I cried mostly every day. I even prayed aloud for a miracle, to make my father and best friend, as well as my idol, better again. How comes I could save the lives of others, but not save my own father? Our family regrouped and we supported each other. It was so difficult explaining to the kids just how sick my dad was.

He was taken into hospital and undertook radiotherapy and other tests showed his cancer was also in his pelvis. We were given false hope at one point they operated on it, we thought there was still a glimmer of hope for him. The hospital was at the end of my road, so I would be up there as much as I possibly could to see him. At home, he was laying on an air mattress and he would constantly try to lift himself off of his backside to help alleviate the pain levels, his closed hands were white where he clenched his fists so tight, which indicated to me that he was in a lot of pain.

The Real Life of Brian??

We didn't really talk, I would just look at him, he would raise his eyebrows occasionally. He'd ask me to take him for a cigarette though, much to the sister of the wards disgust, for I would take him into the toilet, cover up the smoke detector temporarily while he had a quick puff. I wasn't going to deny a dying man his wish for a cigarette. We'd get the odd telling off.

The time element was even more apparent to me at the moment, for I knew my dad only had days before his life would be taken from him. I'd still cry every day, but not in front of him. Some days I could hardly see to drive through my tears. As per his wishes, we were able to get dad back home and we were given aids to help, such as an air bed, commode and walking aids. Not that he was very mobile anyhow. Between my ma, my brother and my sister, we helped to nurse him.

I ended up breaking my leg on a night out with my friends as they tried to rally me round for my birthday. I wasn't really feeling up for going out to be honest, I was like a ticking time bomb. As I've already mentioned, I like to do impressions of famous people and my friends were encouraging me to do some in this pub. There was a group of corporate people out for the night and they were also coercing me to do some impressions.

As the day drew on, a doorman or security guard started his shift ready for the night. He kept coming over to me to tell me to be quiet, as I was disturbing others, which wasn't the case. In fact, I was being egged on. In the end I told him to "Fuck off out of my face" which didn't go down too well. So, I was told to go, I ended up running up some steps and my foot folded back on itself, resulting me snapping my leg in two places.

I found this out by getting home on two trains, a bus and early in the morning after the alcohol wore off. The upside to this, was that I could spend precious time with my dad, that I wouldn't able to otherwise. Although I did struggle to lift him in and out of the bed, as my ma's back was still bad. I think that's partly the reason my leg hasn't healed correctly, but I have no regrets. My partner Tara was very supportive, for even though she had her own problems with her gran having cancer, she'd urge me to go and stay to look after my dad.

We as a family worked as a team to nurse my dad, getting his medicine from the chemist, cooking and caring for him. I'd normally do a lot of the nights, then my brother sister and ma used to do during the day. Palliative nurses would also come in to monitor his ketamine and morphine. I wish I could say that they made him pain free, but they didn't. I think the drugs frustrated him more than anything.

Even when his brothers and sisters came to see him once, they knew he was dying. He would slam his arm down on the bed, especially at one of his brothers who had in previous years stood against dad in small claims court for monies that were once owed to him, that equated to over thirty thousand pounds. Thankfully the next time I saw him was at my dad's funeral, if I had my way, he wouldn't have been there.

My dad was now at the point where the grandkids were kept away from visiting. We wanted them to remember their Grandad through the good times. I'm still getting over the horrific things that I experienced whilst looking after him, feeling helpless to help him as he was yelling in agony. I even had to put his catheter back in where he pulled it out and put my fingers in his mouth to grab one of his teeth that had fallen out. I was coming to the terms that he did not have long to go.

He had lost a lot of weight, his soul seemed to be ebbing away, his readable facial expressions by his eyebrow raising and smile diminished.

My brother, sister and ma would often give each other a cuddle of love and encouragement. Lorraine, my eldest sister, took a massive responsibility of dad's financial affairs and power of attorney.

I think I never told my dad that I loved him or gave him a kiss, as much as I did in the last month of his existence. We never had that sort of relationship. That never bothered me, for I knew he worshipped the ground that his kids walked on. Lorraine probably got the closest to that, he'd often go rigid if you attempted to hug hum. Only ma he would kiss or give a cuddle, but it was normally on his terms.

We managed to keep him home for Christmas. Even though we were all thankful, he was here at home, we were all facing the realization it would be his last. It was difficult to remain upbeat. It sounds awful, but I often watched him at night, writhing in agony or crying out and thinking I should end his life so he wouldn't suffer any further.

It wasn't fair that he as a person lived a life of suffering and torment.

He tried everything he could, to give us a better life, despite having to sacrifice so much in his. I still had another idol in my life, that was my grandad, but as much as I hate to say, my dad was a country mile ahead of him.

The New Year came and there was nothing hopeful about a happy one for us all. The life and soul of my father was nearly sucked from him. His pain levels went through the roof, his medication was slightly altered, but a miscalculation of Ketamine and Morphine made his pain unbearable.

I was struggling to lift him in and out of bed without hurting him, so it was time for him to stay in St Raphaels Hospice.

I came across a book called 'The Occulatum' it was a book of old proverbs that could be read back to front. It originated from people that survived the Great Fire of London. I used to open it randomly and read the saying printed on that page, some were easy to understand, others needed a bit of thought. I think it helped to distract me a little.

The visiting hours were fairly flexible at St Raphaels, we tried to avoid their routine of the doctors rounds or the nurses attending my father for a wash. I still tried to keep him occupied, I even took him to the pub, just down yonder, but it was getting harder, plus I still had my leg in plaster. That was trivial compared to my dad's situation. I'd even bring him in a joint to help him, although one time I got told off by the sister as the smell was wafting down the corridor.

The palliative nurses and doctors were amazing, they reduced the pain levels my dad was feeling, which reduced our anxieties. However, he became less coherent, we were regularly updated on what was happening and what to expect. We knew we didn't have long with him now, that anxiety and sadness will always be etched in my mind. Our family was very close, which I am truly thankful for, plus I had a very supportive partner.

I spent as much time as I possible could at the hospice, I just sat and watched him, his life ebbing away. You still pray for a miracle that wasn't going to happen. I'd look at my ma and give her a hug, it was draining her. It was a long time I'd seen my mum like this.

We were asked to sit with one of the doctors that looked after dad and we were told the news that dad didn't have very long left, in fact he had only hours. His oldest brother came to see him and we were all permitted to be by his side as his time on this earth was nearing the end. He had what they call the 'Death rattle', it was the most peaceful I'd seen him over his illness, although he still looked like he had an anxious look on his face.

It was like all you could hear was his breathing, it became a lot slower. I held his hand, something I hadn't done since I was a child. It was pretty cold, his breathing got a lot slower, then suddenly it paused momentarily, then he started again. It seemed like he shook his head like he didn't want to go.

I remember leaning forward with tears in my eyes, saying to him that he should let go and go and look after Gillian. I kissed him on his forehead and told him I loved him and with that he took his last breath. So, he finally passed away on the 20th of January, 2005 at ten minutes to eight.

I kid you not, something really spooky happened immediately after. The wind suddenly picked up, it seemed like hurricane speed, then there was a massive clap of thunder. Even my uncle looked at me, as if to say "What the fuck?". Maybe it was dad's last parting sign, for he definitely didn't want to go, being only 58 years of age.

We called in the doctor and she confirmed that dad had died. We all gave my ma a cuddle, she'd lost her rock, her soulmate. I'd lost my best mate and my number one idol. At least he wasn't in pain any more.

We had quite a small, modest funeral service for him, as he would have wanted and something was placed in memory of him by Gillian's side. He was the major keystone in our family.

It is said that the pain of losing someone gets better over time, I'm not really sure about that. It has been twenty years to date of me writing this and I still feel that sadness and sorrow to the same extent as I did back then.

I think my Ma did amazing in finding the strength to carry on, she did have support from myself, my sister and brother. I think it was me out of all my family members that was hit the hardest by his death.

My mate Andy supported me at work where I missed him the most. I kept crying a lot, Andy knew how much it meant to me that my dad was gone. I got to the point where I did not want to be an electrician any more. I could still smell him on his tool bag. I kept some of his tools in a box, it's like my shrine for him. I had half of his tools stolen on a site one, for those that stole it, they never meant anything to them. But to me, they were pieces of a puzzle of my dad's life.

He was very touchy about his tools and you were privileged if he let you borrow them.

We have not long had to sort through his belongs as we had to sell our childhood home, which my dad amazingly managed to buy and keep hold of. Our mum has now sadly passed away, she did well to carry on for the last eighteen years without him to be fair.

They are now together again and are without doubt watching over us. Our family tree is able to grow with a lot of thanks to my parents, especially my dad.

He never gave up, no matter what life threw at him. I try not to complain about things because of how my dad was, he just got on with it. People often say that I am the spitting image of my dad, I do have some of his ways, although my persona is more like that of how my Mum was. I try to be like how my dad was, very difficult shoes to fill.

So now you can see the true life of Brian, as how I saw him and what an amazing man he was. A lot of his mysterious ways unveiled, which may not have been apparent to some who knew him.

Bless you dad! One day we will see each other again, you will never be forgotten until then.

You will always be our hero.

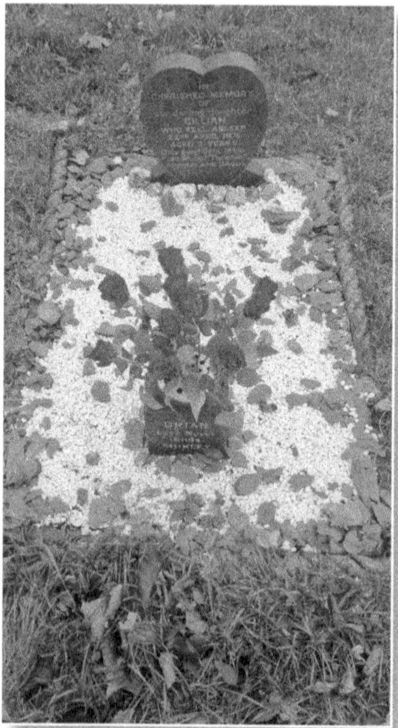

About the Author

I WROTE THIS BOOK DEDICATED to the memory of one of the bravest men I know. I am extremely lucky to have had him as my father. His modesty, determination and bravery have made me strive to be as much like him as possible. I hope the memory of who he was is fairly well depicted in my book and will last eternally to inspire my readers. The biggest hero, much loved and greatly missed.

www.ingramcontent.com/pod-product-compliance
Ingram Content Group UK Ltd.
Pitfield, Milton Keynes, MK11 3LW, UK
UKHW011925010725
460304UK00002B/2